Advan

"Every chapter in _Lyfe_
seeking to live their live intentionally."

--Linda Luecke, Executive Director,
Cornerstone Pregnancy Services

"So what makes life truly worth living? Ask Timothy Michael Olney because he knows. _Life Positive_ serves up the timeless values that bring out the best in each of us in bite-size pieces. Page by page, you'll begin to discover in your own life the difference between what seems urgent at the time and what is truly important."

--Len Howser, Afternoon Drive Time Host,
WFHM 95.5 "The Fish", Cleveland

"_Life Positive_ by Tim Olney is "chucked full" of inspiring thoughts, motivational principles and just plain "good sense" that would help anyone approach each day with a view toward living a more positive life. I would recommend it as a great devotional or inspirational thought for the day!"

--Dr. Bill Mouer

Life
Positive

A treasury of life-enriching
ideas, thoughts and strategies

Timothy Michael Olney

Leaderbrook
PUBLICATIONS

Library of Congress Control Number: 2002092527

All Scripture quotations in this book are from the New International Version of the Bible (NIV) © 1995 by the International Bible Society.

ISBN 0-9719079-0-0

It is not the intent of the author to diagnose, prescribe, or dispense medical advice. The author recommends you consult your doctor before any form of diet or exercise be started. The author assumes no responsibility for your actions.

Life Positive may be purchased for educational, business, or sales promotion use. To obtain quantity pricing, please contact: Leaderbrook Publications, P.O. Box 864, Amherst, OH 44001

DEDICATION

First and foremost, I'd like to thank you, God, for *everything* you've done for me. If it weren't for you, my fulfilling life wouldn't be possible. I long for the day I'll see you in heaven.

I'd like to express my sincere gratitude to the most wonderful person in my life—my wife Jean. Thank you for your unwavering devotion to our marriage, your loving support in all I do, and for all the joys and pleasures you bring to me. You will *always* be the love of my life and my best friend.

To my father, for being my hero. Your steadfast faith and devotion to your family and to God is something you should be proud of. Thank you for being a great leader, father, and brother in Christ. The Lord has special plans for you on earth and in heaven.

To my mother, for being there at all times. Your love and kindness exemplify the wonderful characteristics of what every mother should be. You'll always have a special place in my heart.

To Nathaniel and Kylie, you touch me so deeply. You are special gifts and beautiful in every way. I can't begin to describe my feelings when thinking of you. May your lives be filled with all things positive.

TABLE OF CONTENTS

ACKNOWLEDGMENTS

My heartfelt thanks go out to my wife Jean for her love and support during the entire project and helping with the final changes.

A very special thanks is due to Scott Brown for his never-ending encouragement, suggestions, and "action-above-all" support. His enthusiasm is contagious and he's one of a kind.

Many people lovingly contributed their advice and thoughts. I thank each of them. I'm especially grateful to Ralph Innocenti, Barb Olney, and Laura Workman, who made suggestions for changes and ideas I would never have realized.

They say you can't judge a book by it's cover and I'd have to agree. If that's true, then this book cover will make this one of the best-selling books of all time. Credit goes to Jason Shaffer for the late nights and changes I put him through.

I also thank Marilyn Weishaar, for doing a great job of editing the rough draft. She helped to put words in order and to narrow my focus.

And last but not least, a very warm and hearty thanks to my final editor, Jerry Buchs. Words can't express the work he did on this manuscript. He was the proverbial icing on the cake. (I probably shouldn't have used the word "proverbial" there, sorry Jerry)

Why I wrote *Life Positive*...

This book has been a goal of mine for many years. It was born out of a desire to help others. If you apply one or more strategies from this book, you'll not only make a remarkable improvement in your life, but consequently, you'll make remarkable improvements in our world, too.

Just what is *Life Positive*? It is:

- Having a sunny attitude, even if the day is gray.

- Picking up trash on the sidewalk, even though you didn't put it there.

- Returning the lost wallet you found with the money still inside.

- Putting your family before work, not vice-versa.

- Being thankful for all that you have.

- Taking control of your own life.

- Giving your best without expecting anything in return.

14

- Making fun and laughter part of every day.

- Realizing that everything—whether it's your life or your work—is about people.

- Understanding that "life may not be easy, but what you make of it is."

- Helping someone in need.

- Leaving the world better than you found it.

- Living well, laughing often, and loving more.

- Reaching for someone's hand and touching their heart.

- Living before you die—not the opposite.

Are you living a positive life?

Introduction

If you're like me (and you probably are) you've always wanted a meaningful life. Everyone wants an extraordinary life—one that gives you extra time, less stress, more balance, better relationships, and increased happiness—a life filled with unbridled enthusiasm. That's what I hope *Life Positive* will do for you.

As you travel down the path of your journey called life, you need to realize there will be bumps and detours along the way. But the key to a positive life is to not let these difficulties stop your progress. Too many people are miserable, unhappy in relationships, and doing work they don't love. Too many are being, not living. I believe there are two ways of dealing with unfortunate circumstances: you either alter the circumstances or you alter the way you deal with them.

Life may not be easy, but *what you make of it* is. And that, my friend, is what really matters. In order to make lasting improvements in your life, you must begin on the *inside* in order to change on the outside.

The desire to be happy and successful, to have a positive and fulfilling life, is deeply rooted within your heart. *Life Positive* will show you how to look inside yourself and make those desires become realities. It offers insight, hope, energy, and a wealth of useful strategies that will give you the power to change whatever you want to change. You'll feel inspired about your life and excited about your future.

In today's fast-paced world, too many people are content to look for a magic quick-fix or a pill to swallow; we look to science or technology for the answers on how to live a great life. The personal touch has been left in the dust. We've forgotten that life is about people—and it will *always* be that way.

Principles and insights into living have been with us since God created man. They haven't changed. They are always there, either working for us or against us. The positive choice is to make them work *for* us.

In this book, I'm going to share with you some powerful strategies to improve the way you live. You will learn how to awaken each day with a new outlook. You'll be excited about the day ahead. You'll have a new passion for living.

There are four things you must do before reading this book:

1. You must admit that you could use some improvement in some area of your life, whether it is in your career, attitude, relationships, happiness, finances, health, family, etc.

2. You must accept the idea that this author has something valuable to share.

3. You must admit that if the ways you've been searching for happiness, success, or peace of mind haven't

been working, you must change. Or, as the farmer said: "If you don't like the crop you're reaping, check the seed you're sowing."

4. You must admit that no one else is going to change your life for you—only you can do that. And then you must act. All of the wonderful thoughts, insights, and tools of self improvement are useless until they are implemented. Good intentions don't get the job done. Ask yourself, "What do I have to lose if I follow the ideas and strategies from *Life Positive* that will help me discover a better way to live?"

When God gave you authority over this world, he also gave you authority over yourself. You create your own life. God has never controlled you. Instead, He has given you intelligence, vision, and talent to mold your own journey through life.

The key of course is *choice*. With so many options in life, why do so many people spend their days worrying about everything, wallowing in self pity, poverty, or unhappiness? They haven't figured out that they have choices, and they continue to make excuses.

In your lifetime, you'll make thousands of choices. You have a choice right now. You can choose to put this book down or you can choose to browse through these pages to find ways that will enrich your life.

Life Positive comes from more than twenty years of studying successful people, fellow employees, my friends and family, books, the Bible, and my own experience. It is based on real life, not theory. The majority of what you'll read here is the result of personal experience, good and bad.

My heartfelt wish is that this book will cause a chain reaction of positive thoughts, events and outcomes in your life. I hope that you will be able to look back in forgiveness, look forward with high expectations, and look up with thankfulness.

Whether you want to increase your happiness, enhance a relationship, improve your career, or just create the kind of life you've always wanted, when you begin to use the strategies in this book, your life will be truly enriched.

Timothy Michael Olney

CHAPTER

1

Living from the inside out

And you're off!

When *War Emblem* won the 128th running of the Kentucky Derby in 2002, it was probably his heart that made the difference. Obviously, no one physically saw *War Emblem's* heart that day. They only saw what it produced—a winner.

Studies show that average horses have hearts that weigh around seven pounds. The great thoroughbreds—the exceptional ones—have huge hearts, hearts that weigh from 10 to 24 pounds. The theory is that bigger hearts pump more oxygenated blood, thus helping the horses run faster longer, and giving them a better chance to win. Of course, not all horses with huge hearts claim first place. But the odds are in their favor.

Wouldn't it be wonderful if the same were true for us humans? The bigger our hearts, the better our chances of being counted among the winners? Of course I am not talking about the physical size of the human heart but the intangible size, the size that makes some people larger than life when measured in good deeds rather than in those things we can see, touch, or count.

Too often we look at the size of a person's bank account, their executive title, or celebrity status to determine life's winners. That's not the way it should be.

When judgment day is upon us, do you think our destinations will be determined by the size of our wallets? Not likely.

In life, a person with a big heart is always a winner; someone without never is.

"It is not genius nor glory that reflects the greatness of a person; it is the heart."

Check to see if you have a heart problem

You can tell a lot about what's in a person's heart by listening to his words and watching his actions. There are two kinds of hearts when it comes to the human species. One is the pump that keeps the blood flowing; the other is a person's true character and inner feelings.

A person who often lies, talks negatively about others, and treats people unfair, is often described as mean-hearted. On the other hand, someone whose actions are kind, encouraging, and truthful is said to be kind-hearted.

Your heart is like a fruit-bearing tree. People recognize the tree by the fruit it produces. The same can be said for people. A great person produces great things from a great heart.

However, you can't solve your heart problems just by cleaning up your words and actions. You must fill yourself with new life-enriching attitudes and motives.

The easiest way to check for a heart problem is to look at your actions and to listen to your words. What kind of fruit do you produce?

Make it your goal to produce great fruit each day.

True giving is not a trade-off

Many of you have a hard time giving because you're previous attempts at giving were often misunderstood. When things haven't worked out, you remember being disappointed, used, or victimized, and you are no longer confident in your ability to give.

However, were you really giving or were you trading? The latter is most likely true. You were probably playing the "I'll scratch your back if you scratch mine" game. Trading favors is not giving—it's an act of focusing on your own return. There's nothing wrong with trading favors if you make that clear from the beginning.

True giving is different. It doesn't focus on what the return will be. True giving focuses on doing something for someone else—*without* conditions. Giving never looks back. It moves forward.

The true giver doesn't give for the joy it brings to him or her. The true giver already has that joy and wants to share it with others. It's the joy that energizes the act of giving.

When giving, don't expect anything in return.

Dare to be first

People who think the world owes them something often believe life is unfair. They never want to risk anything or say they're sorry for things they've done. They never want to go first in a relationship or situation because they fear they might get hurt. Their attitude reflects one thought—"I'll give to them only if they give to me."

Do you want to improve a friendship or relationship? Don't wait for the other person to come to you. Think about it like a four-way stop. If four drivers reach the intersection at the same time and everyone waits for the other person to go first, no one will get through the intersection. Someone has to go first.

Think of yourself as a driver. Make the first move. Get through that intersection. See how good life is on the other side. Don't wait for someone else to make the first move.

It's easy to create a more joyful relationship. Make a list of all the important people in your life—family, friends, or co-workers. When you have a few spare moments, pull out your list. Make a phone call. Write a short note. Send an e-mail. Encourage them, leave an inspiring message, or drop by just to say "Hi!" Eventually, these little positive actions will become part of your routine.

Do something because your heart tells you to, not because you expect something in return. What you do doesn't need to be expensive or take a lot of time. Remember, "It's the thought that counts."

Whenever you think of your list, I encourage *you* to take action and do something positive. You'll be glad you did. At least three things will happen:

1. You'll feel confident and peaceful when you think of the important people in your life.
2. You'll reap the rewards of joy, peace, and the satisfaction of knowing you made someone else's life a little brighter, at least for the moment.
3. Your relationships will be strengthened and the bond you forge will continue to grow.

Take the initiative and do something positive.

CHAPTER

2

Core Values

Mobile homes don't attract tornados

When I was discharged from the U.S. Marine Corps, I decided to move to Myrtle Beach, South Carolina. I couldn't afford a traditional house, so I opted for one with wheels. I lived in a mobile home.

I was fortunate enough to never experience the destruction of a tornado first hand, but I've seen the aftermath on television. When a tornado sweeps through a mobile home park, there's generally nothing left except for the cement pads they were on.

After mobile homes are towed to a site, they are placed on cement blocks and the wheels are removed. The homes are strapped to a cement pad or tied down with soil anchors. In some cases skirting is added around the bottom. Generally, there is little or no foundation.

Traditional houses, on the other hand, are built on a basement or foundation, making the dwelling an extension of the ground. Although permanent houses can be—and sometimes are—destroyed by the ferocity of a tornado or another of nature's violent fits of temper, the majority will withstand stormy weather. The key is the foundation.

The same is true in life. A solid foundation made up of positive core values and philosophies that you can build on keeps you grounded.

Regardless of what bad weather blows in—the economy, personal problems, relationship/marital problems, etc.—the odds that you will be standing when the bad weather is over are greater if you have a strong foundation.

Tornados would still cause destruction even if mobile homes didn't exist. But in life, the chances for survival are much greater if you're living on a well-built foundation—both physically and spiritually.

Start with a strong foundation and build from there.

"Remember, it wasn't raining
when Noah built the Ark."
--Howard Ruff

Be honest with yourself

Anyone can claim to have integrity. But there's a world of difference in claiming to have it and actually having it. Integrity is the cornerstone of character. *It's not something you do; it's something you are*— a person of integrity. You don't have integrity because you do things that are ethical, sincere, and right. You do the right things because you have integrity.

Integrity is who you are when no one else is looking. (When absolutely no one but God knows what you are doing, are you doing the right thing?)

People know you by what they see and hear about you, about your attitudes and your actions. Anyone can put on a false front—*act* in ways that do not represent the real person. Some people are better at it than others. They exude a false sense of integrity when they are in the spotlight.

But what about when the spotlight is turned off? Show me the person who is ethical, sincere, and right when the cameras *aren't* rolling, and I'll show you a person of integrity.

Whether your integrity is real or just a front for others is up to you. Did you know you act upon and become what you think about? Did you know that the human mind can only focus on one thing at a time? If you're continually thinking of positive things, there is less opportunity for negativity to creep in. It's true. You can fill your mind with positive or negative, good or evil. The choice is yours.

It's human nature to have some sort of sinful or evil thoughts. But you can overcome your iniquities by choosing right over wrong, ethics over convenience, and truth over popularity.

So how do you travel the path of integrity in this ever-changing world? You must make better choices while standing by your unchanging principles. Here's a short course in how to become a person of integrity:

- Think about what defines integrity.
- Constantly fill your mind with those things.
- Make sure your actions are consistent with your thoughts.
- Repeat the first step.

Finally, brothers, whatever is true, whatever is noble, whatever is right, whatever is pure, whatever is lovely, whatever is admirable—if anything is excellent or praiseworthy—think about such things.
Philippians 4:8

Don't be like them

You will be consistently disappointed if you expect others to show gratitude for the things you do. Your hard work is most likely appreciated, but very few people will take the time to actually say so.

You can learn an important lesson from people who never convey their gratitude: Don't be like them!

The next time someone does something for you, express your gratitude by writing a note, thanking them in person, leaving a message on an answering machine, or sharing with the person's boss. Your gratitude won't go unnoticed.

Express your gratitude to others every chance you can.

Character cannot be split

Other people determine your reputation--*you* determine your character. Every time you make choices, you are creating and shaping your character.

Lately, there's been a debate about character. Some people think it's possible for a person to possess both a public and a private character. They say what someone does in private is his or her own business, as long as it doesn't affect other people or what the person does in public.

For example, a former U.S. president had intimate relations with someone other than his wife while he was in office. His *whole* life was affected, not just his personal life. His character was tarnished. Still, some people insisted his duties as president had nothing to do with his personal life. They said they didn't care what he did in his personal life, as long as the country was running smoothly. I say its a bunch of baloney.

When you start dividing personality and actions into different categories, you're getting away from the very definition of character. At its core, character is defined by integrity, and integrity is made up of your wholeness. Character and integrity go hand and hand. Wholeness is described as completeness and fullness. Character doesn't mean *part* of your life. It represents your *whole* life.

Who would you rather hire?

- Salesperson A, who sells a ton of your product, but there are repercussions because he compromised your company by bending the truth, cheating, stealing, etc.?

- Salesperson B, who has unquestionable character but may not sell as much of your product?

Quite often, the reason Salesperson A sells a ton of products is because he cheats the system. Who couldn't sell more by cheating? In the long run, if all things are equal, a salesperson with solid character will most often outsell the person without it.

Smart companies that want long-term customer relationships hire Salesperson B. People do business with people who they like and trust. If that trust is broken, so is the relationship.

Whether you are salesperson, plumber, housewife, receptionist, accountant, or work in an ivory tower, your character—good or bad—will eventually help or haunt you.

Do what it takes to develop good character and maintain integrity.

Invite Tim to speak at your next event!

"His mixture of inspiration, motivation, and humor, will enrich your audience!"

"Tim shares from the heart...and it shows!"

Tim's presentations are filled with ideas, strategies, and personal stories that will have you living, laughing, and loving your way to a better life. He is fast becoming one of the nation's most sought after speakers!

Whether you are looking for a speaker to liven-up your next meeting, looking for some motivation for your company, or just want to "relieve the stress" within your group or organization, Timothy Michael Olney will deliver a power-packed presentation.

For more information on Tim's speaking topics, fees, and availability, please visit his website at: www.TimOlney.com or call 1-800-250-1636

Order Tim's Audio Tapes & CD's

"How to Live Your Life Positive"

You've read the book, now enjoy
the audio! Tim shares his ideas,
thoughts, and strategies about life
with you in a way that you'll not
only enjoy, but you'll listen to over
and over again!
Your choice of CD or Cassette. $12.95

---

www.TimOlney.com or call 1-800-250-1636

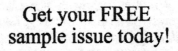

Get your FREE
sample issue today!

Positive Boost Monthly is the #1
pocket-size inspirational magazine.
Each month, this power-packed magazine brings you
ideas, thoughts, stories, quips, and quotes to add a
"positive boost" to your day. Enjoy a sample issue today!

CHAPTER

3

From deep within

Don't lose your passion

Somewhere in the last hundred years people have lost their passion for the things they believe in.

Instead of living before they die, people die before they live. Instead of waking up with a sense of purpose and a fire in the heart, too many men and women began to wake up with dread and apathy for the upcoming day.

It's a shame, but it's true. When was the last time you couldn't sleep because you had a heart-thumping enthusiasm about an idea or belief?

Fortunately for all of us, some people felt and continue to feel that enthusiasm. As a matter of fact, passion can be traced back to the inner core of every great accomplishment.

So how do seemingly ordinary people achieve great things? By harnessing a burning desire and deep-felt intensity toward their goal.

Passion is not a pill. It's not a romance novel. And it's not the centerfold of a magazine. It's not found in a chat room or at the local drug store. It's not something you find. It's something you are.

Passion shapes your existence. It is the energizing force which fuels the fire of your convictions and inspirations. It allows you to express yourself from deep within, on a soul-to-soul basis. Passion is an integral part of enjoying a positive life. Most successful people have become so because of the overwhelming passion and drive they possess.

You can become passionate by digging deep within your soul and sharing your philosophies and beliefs with others. You can become passionate by:

- Showing friends and family you care about them—through your thoughts, and your life.
- Showing customers you care about them in the way you treat, respect, interact, and help them.
- Spending hours and hours on something you love doing.

Being passionate is being real—real in everything you do. You can't lie about it and you can't fake it. Passion allows you to see right through the transparency of material possessions and false securities. When someone is sincerely passionate about what they believe in, you can see it in that person. You can feel the passion transferred to you.

It's also easy to spot a pretender and their lack of sincerity and heartfelt enthusiasm. You can sense the insincerity. You don't see the passion. You don't feel it.

Why should you be passionate? Because passion flows from deep within. It gives you an indescribable pleasure that will transform your innermost feelings into whatever you are doing. And that, my friend, is what it's all about!

Focus not on finding passion but on <u>being</u> passionate.

"Only passions, great passions,
can elevate the soul to great things."
--Denis Diderot

Get high on life

When you do something you love to do—when you are passionate about it—your energy reaches new heights. When you are excited about what you're doing, when you are moving toward a goal with positive expectancy, the only limits on what you can accomplish are those you place on yourself. You'll get high on life.

Want to see impossibilities vanish? Get involved with someone who is passionate about what they're doing. A fire that burns with passion in someone's heart lifts everything in their life. That's why passionate people are so effective. People with a great passion for something and few skills will almost always outperform people with great skills and no passion.

Everyone seems to think successful people have become so because of their education, money, or family tree. While all of these things help, it's really passion that makes the difference between success and failure, between the positive and the negative.

Enjoy life with a passion!

"Sincere and honest change
always starts on the inside."

CHAPTER

4

Happiness, joy, and all that good stuff

The pursuit of happiness

The right to seek happiness is so highly valued that our Founding Fathers wrote it into the Declaration of Independence. It's one of the three inalienable rights: life, liberty, and the pursuit of happiness.

To a degree, happiness (or unhappiness) is a by-product of good (or bad) circumstances, i.e. getting a new car, a raise, good news, etc. (being in an accident, getting fired, etc.).

Most people are conditioned to believe that happiness comes with a big car, house, money, prestige, etc. When you get them, you take them for granted. You expect to be happy, or conversely to be sad when you don't get them.

I believe that when you choose to let circumstances dictate your happiness, you are letting others make decisions for you. And when you do that, you give up some of the power to determine your own life. Happiness is not in your circumstances, but in yourself.

Striving for happiness isn't the problem; expecting it is. There's nothing wrong with reaching out to pluck all the happiness you can from the tree of life. It is wrong, however, to expect to have happiness handed to you like a piece of ripe fruit. You need to realize that like the piece of fruit, your happiness will decay with time if you don't harvest its sweetness.

When you learn to appreciate—not expect—all of the good things that come your way, you will be happier when they do come your way and less dejected when they don't. Remember, the Founding Fathers didn't promise you happiness, only the *pursuit* of it. There's a big difference.

Enjoy life regardless of your circumstances.

"The best way for a person to be happy
is to count his blessings and not his cash."

--Anonymous

Joy to the world

Ninety-nine out of one hundred people would likely say happiness is one of their main goals in life. Happiness is good for everyone. However, you need to understand happiness comes and goes. It's dependent, in part, on your physical well-being. When you feel great, you're more likely to be happy. It's as simple as that.

Your emotions are like a roller coaster. No one feels great all the time. That's why you need *joy* as well as happiness in your life. Joy and happiness aren't one and the same. Happiness is temporary and unpredictable. Joy is permanent and reliable. It is the by-product of a positive, fulfilling life.

True joy is more deeply rooted within you than happiness. Happiness is a delicate flower that can be blown apart by the lightest breeze. Joy is like the mighty oak that stands tall and sturdy against the strongest of winds.

Have you ever been around people filled with joy? You can feel that special something about them; their joy is apparent in everything they do. Joyful people accept that there will be good times and bad. Their attitudes are not based on the situation at hand, but rather on their positive outlook on life.

If you are lacking joy in your life, you may not be looking at life from the right perspective. Perhaps you need to look at life in a blessed rather than a negative way. You need to remember that life is a journey, and there will be bumpy roads and times you will veer off the path. You must accept the fact there will be adversity. It's part of life and it helps build your strength. When it comes, you must change your focus to the positive things instead of dwelling on the negative.

Joyful people are not overcome by their lives—they enjoy life as they overcome.

If you let worry, fear, and stress invade your thinking every time you hit a bump in the road, you'll miss the good things life has to offer.

You can make yourself miserable or happy at any given moment by choosing to focus on the negative or choosing to focus on the positive.

Focus on the positive. You can only think about one thing at a time.

Want joy in your life? Forget external circumstances and focus on positive things.

It's never enough

Many people spend a lifetime seeking what I call the "Three P's": possessions, position, and power. Whether it's a promotion, money, a fancy car, or an award, you tend to think, "What's next?" If that's you, then you suffer from the "never enough" syndrome.

We live in an era that is the wealthiest and the most technologically advanced, and that allows more people than ever the opportunity to have what they want. In this more-of-everything era, one would expect to find everyone as happy as pigs in a mud hole on a hot summer day. But we're not. In fact, we live in an era that is one of the most dissatisfied of all time. We never have enough.

The key to overcoming the never-enough syndrome is learning to be happy with what you have. You should not be so obsessed with what you want that you set yourself up for failure. If your happiness only depends on whether or not you reach your goals or obtain the Three P's, your life will be hollow and empty.

Having everything you want is not bad, nor is striving to reach your goals harmful. But if the desire to have more and more replaces your thoughts of how blessed you are for what you have, you're on the wrong path. If you continue thinking more is better, you'll never be satisfied.

I look forward to more things in life and reaching my goals and dreams just like everyone else. But I'm happy with what I have now. If I don't obtain everything I want, I will still have enjoyed a fulfilling life.

You can spend your energy wanting more and more—or you can appreciate the blessings you already have and move forward.

I encourage you to live every minute with passion toward your goals, kindness in your ways, and thankfulness in your heart..

"Happiness cannot be traveled to, owned,
earned, worn, or consumed. Happiness is
the spiritual experience of living every minute
with love, grace, and gratitude."

--Denis Waitley

"Most folks are about as happy as
they make up their minds to be."

--Abraham Lincoln

CHAPTER

5

Attitude is everything

Live like a child

I'll never forget the breath-taking mountain-top view from Citadel Hill in Halifax, Nova Scotia while attending a seminar a few years ago. The scenery was nothing short of spectacular. But there was something more.

While sitting on a park bench, I noticed a couple of children playing. They weren't just playing; they were having the time of their lives. It made me remember the fun times and carefree attitude I had as a child.

Childhood. What do you remember about your childhood? There were no worries, no fear. You were eager to learn and grow. You were happy to just wake up in the morning. What happened? Where did it all go? Why are you not living life with the enthusiasm of a child?

Healthy young children embrace life with a trusting, happy, venturesome, worry-free energetic view. Why does it have to end? What happens to the young child in you when you grow up?

It's simple, really. You let life take over. You start to go about your daily routine and get caught up in the business of living – working, solving problems, entertaining, acquiring things, and coping with stress and problems. Life seems to spin out of control until you lose touch with those deep heartfelt desires and youthful happiness. Your untroubled past is just that, the past. It's easier to simply go on your way with the same-old, same-old mentality.

It doesn't have to be that way. If you take the worry-free attitude of a child, you can take control of your life and start living again.

In the book *Watermelon Magic*, Wally Amos is quoted as saying, "Obituaries always list the year you were born and the year you died, separated by a dash, 1932-2003. When you were born or when you died is not nearly as important as what you did in between – what you put in your dash."

Enjoy your life while there's still no date at the end of your dash.

The mind is a powerful thing

Have you ever wondered how some people are able to get so much out of life?

Nothing ever seems complicated or difficult for them. They continually succeed in all that they do. They are liked by everyone. They consistently overcome obstacles. If they ever struggle with anything, it never shows.

So how do you become like them? For starters, you need to act as if exciting things will happen to you. You need to adopt an attitude of opportunity. A positive attitude can shape your life because you act according to your expectations.

I know what you're thinking. You're thinking I'm like every other motivational speaker that talks about having a great attitude. Typically when you put a motivational speaker on the platform, you already know what they're going to say.

They say that if you have a good positive attitude, everything in your life will be just fine.

I've lived with that philosophy for the past 30 years and I've still had more bad things happen to me than you could imagine.

Having a positive attitude isn't going to keep anything from happening to you. But it will allow you to interpret what does happen to you. This is one of the most important concepts you must grasp to enjoy life fully. It's not what happens to you, it's your *perception* of what happens to you.

I want you to keep another idea in mind as you read through the remainder of this book: There is no reality, only your perception of reality. Whatever meaning your life has for you will be the meaning you give it. It's an idea so profound, that it influences whether or not you are happy, sad, carefree, or stressed.

A positive mental attitude will propel you to new heights. You'll think differently. Act differently. You'll enjoy life like there's no tomorrow.

There is nothing in this world you cannot do when you put your mind to it. Nothing you cannot be. Nothing you cannot have. Nothing can stop you!

Your destiny changes with your thoughts. I encourage you to become what you wish to become and do what you wish to do.

"Think you can, think you can't;
either way you'll be right."
--Henry Ford

Start your life, don't end it

This may shock you, but statistics say forty people will attempt to kill themselves in the next hour. Why? Because they don't think they have a reason for living. They believe the lies the world tells them. They believe their circumstances control them.

If you look at people that enjoy a happy, serene life, you'll find they almost always have a positive attitude.

If you want a fulfilling life, then a positive attitude is essential. It is not only the basis for your contentment, but it also has a huge bearing on how others interact with you.

Ever been around a negative person? Not an exciting experience, is it? I once worked with a lady that had a negative attitude. Every morning for a year, I said good morning to her in a friendly upbeat voice. She never once said good morning back. She always responded with an emotionless "Hi." That's it. Nothing more.

There is nothing wrong with that simple approach. It's just that she was unhappy about everything *all day*. No one in the office ever wanted to be around her because of her attitude. Who could blame them?

Great attitudes, on the other hand, are contagious. It's easy to be around someone who is positive and happy. It gives a lift to the day no matter what else may be going on. It's especially helpful when you're having a bad day yourself to associate with those who are looking up, instead of down.

When you think about it, we should be the happiest people on earth because we live in a country with so much freedom and opportunity.

What happened to you yesterday, good or bad, and whatever the circumstances, your attitude today is *your* choice. Make it the right one. Remember, it is much easier to smile than it is to frown. Just make sure your face knows about it.

Change your attitude today and you'll have a better outlook for tomorrow.

"It may not be your fault for being down,
but it's got to be your fault for not getting up."
--Steve Davis

The glass is never too full

Imagine sitting down at the kitchen table with a full glass of water in front of you. Here's a question: Can you pour more water into the glass? Even though the glass is completely full to the brim, can you put more in?

The answer of course, is yes. Yes, you can pour more water in, but at the same time it will overflow and soak whatever is around it.

Positive-thinking people are like the glass of water. Their hearts and minds are filled with optimism, and they know there's no limit to what they can take in. There's also no room for negative things that might clutter their lives.

They consistently read books, listen to tapes, attend seminars, and associate with other like-minded people. They strive for plenty of positive information on a daily basis. When they pour more in, their attitudes overflow and touch others.

Life has a never-ending abundance of inspirited things to be poured in. When you are filled to overflowing with these things, there is no room for hate, bad attitudes, pessimism, or the other stuff that gets in the way of living a fulfilling life.

Do yourself a favor and be like the glass.

Your glass can never be too full of the positive.

Stop worrying and start living

I have automobile insurance for two reasons:
1. In case something happens to my vehicles.
2. It's the law.

People that ride in my car think I'm crazy because unless I have something valuable in my car, I leave the keys in the ignition and the doors unlocked. They think I'm nuts!

I think it's great because I don't need to carry around a set of keys. I won't lose them because I know they're in the ignition, and it's also convenient. Besides, who cares if my car gets stolen—I could use a new one anyway.

If a thief wants to steal a car, he's going to get it whether it is equipped with that popular anti-theft device, the latest technologically advanced alarm, or if the keys are in the ignition. Worrying about that possibility is no guarantee that it won't happen.

So I carry automobile insurance—just in case something happens. Isn't that why everyone carries insurance? Just in case?

If something bad is going to happen—loss of a job or significant other, injury, a lousy day, etc.—it's going to happen. Worrying won't stop it!

Do *you* worry too much? Do you worry about the details

over which you have no control, while neglecting specific areas (such as your attitude, your relationships, and your responsibilities) that *are* under your control? Did you know that worrying isn't going to change the outcome?

I do know what worrying *will* do. It'll damage your health, disrupt your productivity, and negatively affect the way you treat others.

Instead of worrying about what you can't control, concentrate on what you can. Oh, and by the way, don't tell my insurance company about my car thing. OK?

Stop worrying and start living!

"Real difficulties can be overcome, it is only
the imaginary ones that are unconquerable."
--*Theodore N. Vail*

You're better than you feel

Don't believe it? Imagine one of those days when nothing goes right. It's a day filled with anger, worry, and emotional pain. It's just plain depressing. Then imagine that suddenly someone walks up to you with a check for ten million dollars. Yes, ten million dollars to keep, invest, or spend, no strings attached.

Suddenly the sky is brighter, problems melt away, and euphoria replaces depression. In the length of time it took for the check to change hands, bad feelings and thoughts were gone.

When your attention is diverted from the negative, your spirit soars and your feelings turn on a dime. It happens all the time.

When a child falls and you know that they may be hurting, the first thing you do is try to divert their attention. You try to get them to think of something else so that they will forget about the bump or bruise.

Professional athletes often play through injury. They feel it, but focus on other things. They know that there is more to themselves the that injured body part. Some athletes perform at their highest level when they're injured. What's the secret? They dig deep within themselves to overcome the pain.

They rise above it and concentrate on the task at hand.

If you want to overcome worry, pain, setbacks, or the way you feel, you must rise above it. You need to shift your thoughts to other things. At first you'll likely experience great resistance because the world tells you to submit to your feelings. It's accepted practice these days.

Yet it doesn't have to be that way. You can get out of this depressing habit if you don't identify with it and don't let it consume you. You can overcome the pain.

What can thinking about the pain do anyway? Will it change the situation?

Don't get me wrong. I'm not talking about ignoring negative things—like a run in with the boss—that require your attention in order to be corrected. I'm just saying don't be controlled by them.

Think about what is good and positive and forget about the negative.

Puttin' on the Ritz

A few years ago, I treated my wife to a romantic dinner, limo ride, and a grand stay at the Ritz-Carlton Hotel. I phoned ahead and asked, "Could you deliver a bowl of strawberries, a candle, and a bottle of non-alcoholic champagne to my room by eight o'clock?"

The employee on the other end answered with an enthusiastic "Absolutely, Mr. Olney. Is there anything else I can do to make your accommodations more delightful?"

I told her that would be all. She assured me we would have a wonderful stay and all my requests would be taken care of. She conveyed an exceptional *caring* attitude throughout the entire 10 minute conversation.

Next I needed to make the transportation arrangements. To my surprise, I received a very rude and almost bitter response from the lady helping me with the limousine reservations. I couldn't believe I was about to give her hundreds of dollars for her services. It didn't even seem like she cared. It was quite a contrast to my earlier phone call.

I'm still amazed at the positive attitudes of *every single* employee I came in contact with at the Ritz-Carlton. I could sense these people truly cared about us as their guests. I'll never forget the way they treated both of us. From the first phone call to the time we checked out, they treated us as if we were royalty.

I wish I could say something positive about the limo company, but I really can't. The lady on the phone was impolite and the limo driver spoiled a few of the surprises I had planned for my wife.

Why is it some people have positive attitudes and others don't? Why is it some people actually *care* about their customers? In the example above, I know which employees receive world-class training on how to care for customers—it's clearly evident. I also know the exceptional customer service reflects the heartfelt philosophy and values of an exceptional organization. The Ritz-Carlton goes to great lengths to hire caring people with caring hearts. What can you learn from both these companies?

In life and in business, attitudes can make a huge difference. Whether at work, at home, or on the road, adopting a caring attitude will brighten up your life and those around you.

Share your caring attitude with everyone.

CHAPTER

6

Fun and laughter

Put fun in your life

When I was a kid, I always got into trouble for having too much fun. My teachers said it was innocent but disruptive. My friends said it was great. My parents said…well, let's not talk about that. I still look back and relive the fun I had as a young child. Today, I'm still a kid at heart—and always will be.

The day you lose your desire to have fun, you become afflicted with a life-threatening disease; it's called negativity. Not life threatening in the sense that you'll die, but in the sense that you won't live. You don't have to look far to find people who have contracted this disease.

Every chance I get, I let myself revert back to the kid in me. While traveling along a country road the other day, I found myself behind a school bus packed full of kids. Most people would think being behind a school bus is a bad thing because the bus is always stopping and it slows them down. It didn't bother me at all. It gave me a chance to be a kid again. I began making faces with the children looking out the rear window. I had a blast and so did they.

Having fun is a great experience. On occasion, I've been known to answer the phone pretending to be someone else. I make prank phone calls (all in good fun) to my friends and relatives. I crack jokes while riding on a silent elevator. My goal is to have fun in everything I do.

Why do so many people, blessed with presumably fortunate circumstances miss out on all the fun, while others struggling under unfortunate circumstances embrace life with smiles on their faces and laughter in their voices? I don't know the answer, but I do know the first group is missing out on a lot.

How do you spot people who put fun in their lives? They:

- Rarely place blame or complain about things.
- Experience good times as frequently as possible.
- Recall the good times, but don't dwell on the past.
- Adjust to change in a positive way.
- Are serious when it's appropriate.

Having fun is a gift you can give to yourself. You have a choice here just as you do with most things in life. You can choose to have fun or not. Faced with this choice, I'll always choose fun. How about you?

Embrace life a little differently today. Enjoy the benefits of laughter and high spirits.

Feel great without alcohol or drugs

Right about now, some of you are tired of being told to laugh more. All this stuff about having a positive attitude and living life with unbridled enthusiasm is putting you a bit on the edge.

I know, you probably think I've lost my marbles. Well, I haven't and I won't stop writing about this stuff because it works.

Getting high on life is fun, natural, and healthy. Laughing actually decreases the body's levels of stress hormones. Sustained laughter stimulates an increased release of endorphins—nature's miracle drug—that in turn diminishes physical and psychological pain. Sounds good, huh?

Laugh, laugh, and laugh some more. In today's fast-paced, high-stress world we could all benefit from stepping back and laughing at things. Laughter is a great—and healthy—alternative to alcohol and drugs.

"A cheerful heart is good medicine, but a crushed spirit dries up the bones."

Proverbs 17:22

CHAPTER

7

Health and vitality

Wake up on the 'right' side of the bed

Studies have proven that waking up to an alarm clock interrupts the body's natural *circadian rhythms*. These interrupted rhythms can negatively affect your mood when you awaken. If you want to improve your odds of being happy in the morning, you should allow yourself the opportunity to wake up on your own—when your body is ready.

I became aware of this approach when I was attending a seminar in Anaheim, California. I was in my hotel room reading a book that explained how to wake up at any desired time. I was intrigued by the possibility of waking up to *my own* alarm clock.

So I followed the steps in the book that evening and, to my surprise, woke up in the morning at the *exact* time I visualized.

Here's what you do. If you want to wake up at a specific time, close your eyes and visualize that specific time in your mind. Concentrate on that time just before going to sleep and say to yourself, "I'm going to wake up at 5:30."

Picture those numbers right in front of your eyes. You might want to experiment by using a back-up alarm until you've adjusted to the change. You will wake up within a few minutes of your envisioned time, if not the exact time.

If this doesn't work the first time, don't be discouraged. Within the first few days, your body's natural alarm will take over.

The results are amazing. The first time this works, there's a new realization of how much you're in touch with your mind. It's an incredible display of how the subconscious mind really works.

Set your own alarm clock and enjoy a great start to your day!

"Motivation is what gets you started.
Habit is what keeps you going."
--Jim Ryun

Put a little more dawn in your life

In Key West, Florida, near the end of the day, people flock to the water's edge for a beautiful attraction—the golden sunset in the Gulf of Mexico.

While vacationing with some friends, my wife and I had the chance to see this picturesque sunset. It was a beautiful end to our day.

Although a sunset is incredible, I'd rather witness a wonderful *sunrise*. There is just something about an inspiring sunrise that seems to usher in new opportunities for the day ahead.

How you begin your morning sets the tone for the entire day. If you wake up late, drag yourself out of bed, or wake up irritable, most likely you will have trouble with the day. If you've ever awakened on the wrong side of the bed, you know what I mean.

Want to get the morning off to a terrific start? Wake up early and do something inspiring before beginning the daily ritual. Exercise, read a motivating book, listen to music, sit on the deck and relax, envision dreams coming true, or just bask in the glory of the sunrise.

I encourage you to meet the sunrise with confidence. Try some visualization techniques. Imagine being in a favorite vacation spot or visualize your perfect day.

Greeting each day with a fresh perspective and new zest for life is a great way to start your morning.

Start the morning out right and fill every minute with right thinking and worthwhile endeavors. Do this and there will be joy for you in each golden sunset.

"To get up each morning with the resolve
to be happy...is to set our own conditions to the
events of each day. To do this is to condition
circumstances instead of being conditioned by them."

--Ralph Waldo Trine

Enjoy an unbelievable healthy feeling

Did you know that what you eat affects how you feel throughout the day? Want to enhance your physical as well as mental well-being? Want to reduce the risk of disease, look younger, sleep better, lose weight, and achieve a higher level of good health?

Your health—like everything else—is your *choice*. The first step in achieving optimum health is making the decision to take responsibility for it. Choose a healthy alternative over an unhealthy one.

The second step is finding motivation—a reason—for the change. If you're like most people, you'll probably pursue a healthier lifestyle for one of three reasons:

1. Your body fails in some manner—you get sick—and you realize you must take care of it.
2. You've been encouraged by other people's success.
3. You want to change your life and/or looks.

Regardless of the reason, I encourage you to attain that incredible healthy feeling. How? Talk to people that currently live a healthy lifestyle. Find out how they're motivated. What do they do? Ask them for advice. Go to the library (or bookstore) and study the books and listen to the tapes. Start eating right. Live the life.

Why?

The quality of your health begins with the quality of the foods that sustain it.

Make a decision to live a healthier lifestyle.

Maybe Mom was right

I've logged thousands of miles flying across the country. When I started flying, I feared my life would go down in flames. I've since discovered the odds of dying in a plane crash are small compared to dying from an obesity-related illness. It's not even close.

According to a U.S. Surgeon General's report, 300,000 Americans die each year from illnesses caused or worsened by obesity. Fewer than 400 a year die in an airplane-related catastrophe. You do the math.

It's estimated that six of ten Americans are overweight or obese. Looking around at most people every day—and glancing in the mirror—it seems logical to me. Within a few years, fat may soon overtake tobacco use as the chief cause of preventable deaths in the United States. And the reason isn't even a mystery. People eat more calories—too often by shunning fruits and vegetables in favor of super-sized junk foods—than they work off.

Remember what Mom used to say: "Make sure you eat your fruits and vegetables."

I wish I had listened to her. Today, health and medical professionals are recognizing what Mom knew all along. Fresh fruits and vegetables as part of a low-fat, high-fiber diet, slow aging, lower blood pressure, combat cancer, relieve arthritis, treat kidney stones, fight ulcers and give us increased health and vitality. When Mom said, "They're really, really good for you," she was right!

Who else agrees with Mom? Specifically the U.S. Surgeon General's Office, the American Cancer Society, the American Heart Association, the American Institute for Cancer Research, and just about everyone else including the family doctor.

So why do most of us opt for chocolate chip cookies, cheeseburgers, french fries, cake, and cans of soda instead of eating foods rich in vital nutrients? Junk food tastes good, is everywhere around us, and is available in a hurry—three things that are important to most people. I love junk food as much as the next guy, but I've just learned to consume it in moderation.

I'm convinced that dietary changes—in particular, making sure you get large amounts of fresh fruit and vegetable juices—is the key to optimum health and vitality. They'll boost your energy level, enhance the healing power of your body, and supercharge your immune system. What more could one want in terms of health?

Pass on the fries and grab the fruit.

It's in the juice

Jay Kordich, well known as the Juiceman, and the author of *Juicing for Life,* says juicing is a great way to add fresh fruits and vegetables to your diet. It is scientifically proven and is without a doubt one of the best ways to strengthen the immune system, increase energy, lose fat, reduce the risk of disease, and achieve a glowing complexion.

Juicing quickly and efficiently provides the body with the most easily digestible and concentrated nutritional benefits of fruits and vegetables. It's an incredible way to achieve optimum wellness.

When I began juicing on a daily basis a few months ago, the results were amazing. Within the first couple of weeks, my physical health became vastly improved. How?

- My sinuses and nasal passage began to clear within the first few days.
- I was having a lot of headaches before I started juicing and the headaches went away.
- I felt better in the morning because I had more restful sleep.
- I lost my cravings for most of the junk food I was consuming.
- I had boundless energy.

- I lost over 12 pounds in 30 days.
- I felt refreshed and revitalized and as a result, my attitude improved.

I now consider myself a juiceaholic. I'm addicted to the mouth-watering tastes and the incredible results. Yes, I eat other foods. But I make sure I consume at least sixteen ounces of juice each day. It's become a way of life.

Want to get started juicing? Visit *www.PositiveBoost.com.* The website has free juice recipes, comparison guides for juicers, answers to frequently asked questions, and best of all makes available a free guide to getting started in juicing. It offers gallons of information for the person new to juicing.

Juice today, feel results tomorrow.

Take a hike (And enjoy the outdoors)

There really is a magic drug after all. It doesn't require a doctor's prescription. It produces an awesome feeling. It's legal and, best of all, it's free. It provides you with a youthful vitality, which in turn gives you a new outlook on life.

So what is this wonder drug?

Endorphins--the body's own natural morphine.

How do you get these incredible endorphins?

You get moving! Endorphins are chemicals released by the brain when you exercise. The results are fantastic. People who exercise become alert, feel more confident, and think more clearly.

No weight-loss program concerned with your health is going to work for you without exercise.

It's been proven that the more exercise you get, the less time you spend in front of the doctor. As someone once wrote, "If you don't find the time to exercise, you'll have to find the time for illness." Is it any wonder why the majority of people who are obese have more physical problems than those who exercise on a regular basis?

While I'm talking about a healthy lifestyle, a couple other things deserve your attention: fresh air and sunshine. Few people realize how much life-sustaining nourishment our bodies receive from the air we breathe and the sunlight we take in. Clean air and sunshine are valuable life forces.

There's also a misconception going around today that the sun is dangerous. I think the people sharing this information are forgetting that the sun is one of the greatest sources of life on earth. Without the sun, things wither and die.

I'm not saying you should abuse sunshine because we all know that too much of it can burn you. I am recommending that you bask in the life-giving nutrients it provides!

Without a doubt, physical exercise combined with fresh air and sunshine play a crucial role in the realization of great health and vitality. For optimum health, you need to exercise. Whether it's going for a hike, running a 5K, swimming, bike riding, or just going for a walk, the key is to get moving.

Exercise is the key to improved health and fitness.

CHAPTER

8

God and you

God's stadium has unlimited seating

The Cleveland Indians hold the longest consecutive sell-out streak in Major League Baseball. The team chalked up a record 455 sellouts at Jacobs Field in the mid 90's. You couldn't find an empty seat. Then the Indians started to lose more games than usual and ticket requests declined, seats became available, and the streak ended.

Local radio talk show hosts began saying Cleveland fans were fair-weather fans—people that are only interested when the team is winning. It's the truth, but Cleveland doesn't corner the market on fair-weather fans. All professional sports have the same type of fans. When a team is lousy, the only spectators in the stadium are the die-hard fans.

The true fans—some call them fanatics—cheer for their team regardless of how they're playing. They stick with the team whether they finish first or worst. In a perfect world, everyone would be that loyal. But no one ever promised us a perfect world.

It isn't just sports teams that have fair-weather fans. Too often, people are part-time fans when it comes to God. The sad truth is that most people cry out for God only in desperate times. They only fill seats in His stadium when times are rough. They only reach for Him when they have an emergency or frantic request.

That's not the way God intended it. He wants to help and guide you at *all times*—regardless of the circumstance. He doesn't want you to be a fair-weather fan. He wants you to be an all-weather fan. His stadium always has a seat for you. At times it may be only half full, but unlike some soldout stadiums, His arena has unlimited seating.

I encourage you to keep God in your heart and mind. If you do, your life will take on new meaning. Whether you are winning or losing, your life will be better with Him, rather than without.

Don't wait! I encourage you to put your trust in God today.

It's not about the marble floors

Driving around town one day, I couldn't help but notice the many different kinds of churches. There are big ones, small ones, extravagant ones, thrifty ones. There are Baptist churches, Catholic churches, Pentecostal churches, Presbyterian churches, Methodist churches, Lutheran churches, non-denominational churches, and so many others. I lost count of the variety of places to worship in my small town alone.

I don't see a problem in having different names, sizes, and ways of doing things. Differences are good. As a matter of fact, it shows the diversity of people everywhere.

Sometimes, people tend to lose sight of the ultimate goal— to get into heaven. If you do reach that glorious destination, does it really matter if your church was in a basement or housed in a cathedral? Does it really matter if you believe one thing and those who attend the church on the other side of town believe another? Shouldn't we be united in the work of sharing the word of God with others?

God sees no distinction between big or small, black or white, rich or poor, Catholic or Protestant. Why should you? When it comes time to pass through those pearly gates, it won't matter if your church has marble or sand on the floor.

Remember, the Bible doesn't say there will be only a certain number of people or only those who come from a certain kind of church in heaven. The Bible tells us there will be a great multitude that no one can count, from every nation, tribe, people, and language.

God has invited you to join Him in heaven—regardless of your flooring.

Focus on your own relationship with God.

Read a best-seller

My favorite book—the Bible—is the best selling book of all time. No other book comes close. Why? The Bible is based on positive living and life-enriching philosophies. It's a veritable storehouse of promises—over seven thousand of them. Every great inspirational self-help book that has ever been written is based on Biblical principles.

I find the Bible invigorating. But many people are overwhelmed by the thought of sitting down and reading it from cover to cover. I suggest breaking down the Bible into small bite-sized pieces. The important thing is not how many chapters you read or how often you read, it's what you get out of it that really matters.

I encourage you to read the Bible. Whether it's early in the morning or just before bed, read when you can sit-down, relax, and focus on the words. Try to grasp at least one nugget of inspiration that you can apply during the day.

The focus should be on the content and the lessons it offers, not on how fast you can finish it. It's the quality, not the quantity of its pages.

If you have a Bible, read it. If you don't have one, get one.

Communication *with* God

Many people believe that effective prayer is talking *to* God. But effective prayer is talking *with* God. It is a private conversation between an individual and God. It involves listening as well as talking. Communication is a two-way connection.

People often believe they can't hear the voice of God or that God has never spoken to them because they don't know how to listen to and hear God's word.

Most often when you hear God, it's not with your ears, but with your heart and soul. When you learn how to listen, you hear Him more. Your relationship with God is, after all, a two-way relationship.

In his best-selling book *The Prayer of Jabez*, Bruce Wilkinson shows you how daily prayer can help you leave the past behind and break through into the life you were meant to live. He says that when you are sincere and expectant, God will release His miracle power in you. And for all eternity, He will lavish on you His honor and delight.

When you make daily effective prayer a routine part of your life, you begin to notice positive changes. Positive changes will become life-enriching habits.

Make effective prayer a daily habit.

CHAPTER

9

Generalities

Smelly socks in Africa

I had the pleasure of witnessing first-hand the awesome magnitude of Africa's Mount Kilimanjaro. After a half-day African safari, I ventured into the city of Kenya and noticed local craftsmen everywhere. One of them came over, lifted my pant leg, and revealed my white sports socks with red stripes. He led me over to his products and offered to trade me a hand-carved elk in exchange for my socks.

I thought to myself, "You've got to be kidding. He doesn't want the shirt off my back, he wants the smelly socks off my feet!"

The area of Kenya I visited was extremely poor. Owning a pair of American socks (or any socks, for that matter) was a true privilege. The living conditions were a stark contrast to the lofty heights and spectacular view of the world-famous mountain.

The poverty-stricken people of Africa made me realize how thankful I should be, thankful for the country I live in, the food I eat, the air I breath, and oh yeah, the socks on my feet.

You may live in the worst apartment building or the least desirable part of town. But remember, some people don't even have roofs over their heads. You may complain about the holes in your socks, but some people don't even own socks.

As you carry on your day-to-day activities, I encourage you to be thankful for everything you have. Be thankful and blessed in every way. You may not like your life right now, and you may not have everything you want, but bad circumstances happen to all of us. The attitude you have about those bad circumstances is what really matters.

When you take your first breath in the morning, you should be thanking God for making it possible. You should be thankful for every ability, gift, talent, and opportunity that lies within you and before you.

And if you're ever visiting Kenya and see a nice fellow wearing red-striped socks, tell him I said hello.

Be thankful for everything you have.

The richest man in the cemetery

From all outward appearances, you're doing pretty well. You've got a nice car, big bank account, and a nice place to live. Friends and neighbors would probably agree that you work hard and are basically a nice person. You're on your way to becoming successful—making good money and attaining all those material things you've always wanted.

But the truth is you're unhappy. You're empty on the inside and faking it on the outside. None of the material things you've accumulated has brought you joy and happiness. You're probably thinking, "If only I had more money, or a nicer house, or a better job." If only…If only…

There's nothing wrong with having lots of money and material things. As long as you don't believe the myth that you can soar to the pinnacle of prosperity and your life will be transformed into living bliss.

In the end, you'll be measured by your standard of life, not your standard of living. And I don't think anyone will really care if you're the richest in the cemetery.

The misguided opinion that material things will bring you fulfillment is a virus draining your soul of joy, peace, and a meaningful life.

94

Adopt a caring attitude

In his ground-breaking book, *Service with Purpose*, Scott Brown shares how, over time, the concept of customer service has been broken into small pieces of new philosophies. It seems most people have forgotten about the importance of a solid foundation.

He says that these new ideas are only small pieces of the whole puzzle. Companies seem to forget that business is about people and a solid foundation should be based on that belief. And since business is about people, then customer service is about *caring* about the people you do business with.

Shouldn't we look at life the same way? Absolutely. Life is about people. Let's take it one step further, like Scott does.

If life is about people, then living a positive life is about *caring* about people.

So how do you care about others? Here's a few ideas to get you started: Keep in mind that caring is being kind, generous and helpful to everyone. Show people you care by having compassion and empathy and by keeping their best interests in mind. Put their wants and desires above yours.

Whether it's your neighbor, co-worker, or a stranger, show that you care.

Rotten apples' and grousers

Let's face it, some things are discouraging. You don't get a raise. The weather is nasty outside. A relative faces health problems. You get stuck in traffic.

Negativity is natural in circumstances like these. But some people are habitually negative in all situations. They're chronic complainers, grumblers, and whiners. They feel that even if they did try, they couldn't make life better anyway. Here's their two choice words, "why bother?"

I don't believe you should have to endure those rotten apples' and grousers who always seem to be hopeless and helpless.

So what should you do? First, don't react! Step back and recognize that they aren't speaking the truth, only their perception of the truth. Second, listen for the message behind the words. Keep in mind that most of their anger is usually mis-directed.

You then need to offer to explore different solutions. You need to ask permission to participate in the problem-solving process. The idea is to have the negative person assume responsibility for finding a solution.

Periodically, you'll run across someone who, like an old dog with a bone, just won't let go. In that case, do what you can and enjoy your own life regardless of their limited vision.

Don't allow grousers to ruin your day.

Check the facts before pointing fingers

Dubbed as "Michigan's Little Bavaria," the town of Frankenmuth has the prestige of delighting more than three million visitors annually. While taking in a three-day pleasure trip, my wife and I enjoyed the restaurants, the shopping, the Christmas festivals, the tours, and of course the world famous Bronner's Christmas Wonderland store. Anyone who loves Christmas and old-fashioned, fun-loving people, will love this place. I recommend it whole-heartedly.

While staying at a local bed and breakfast inn, we arose one morning prepared to enjoy a country breakfast prepared by the owners. While waiting to partake in this feast, I smelled a foul odor coming from under our table. I immediately blamed my wife Jean, because no one else was around. The smell filled the room. It was worse than rotten eggs.

A few minutes later, the owner apologized because it was her poodle that was passing gas under the table. I then felt bad for accusing Jean before first checking out the situation.

We still laughed and enjoyed the moment. Hey, don't blame the dog, he didn't know any better.

I learned two things from this experience:

       1. Don't put blame on someone without knowing all the facts.

2. Don't "break wind" while at the breakfast table.

How many times have you blamed others without investigating the facts, the circumstances, and the situation? How many times were you wrong?

If you live your life without pointing fingers all the time, I commend you. If that area of your life could use some improvement, I encourage you to improve.

Check it out before pointing fingers.

Just pick up the phone

The other day, I called a friend I haven't talked to in quite a while. It was one of those calls requesting a favor. Suddenly he asked, "Why do you only call me when you need something?"

Boy, did that hurt! He hit me right where I needed it the most. He spoke the truth. It just so happened that the last few times I called him, I was always asking for something—looking for help. It was wrong and I knew it.

When was the last time you called a friend just to say "Hi?" Or the last time you called someone to find out how they were doing?

I always strive to touch base with others for no reason, but sometimes I fall short of that goal. The above incident was a harsh reminder of how I continually need to improve.

What about you?

Call someone because you care, not because you need something.

Cruelty and kindness

Most people believe that today's society is full of cruelty, yet people have been cruel since the beginning of man. We just didn't hear as much about it. Today's increased media coverage and rapid advances in technology leave no stone unturned to attract readers or viewers.

When reading the newspaper or watching television, it's hard to find stories about acts of kindness. Negative news always outsells the positive. That's why any act of kindness, no matter how small, is special. Kind things come from a kind heart. Kind hearts are the foundation of a changed society.

How will you have an effect on society?

Perform random acts of kindness.

Practice a little 'Humbility'

You know the type. They're kind to others and shout about it. They give to the church and tell everyone about it. They perform acts of kindness and make sure someone knows it. Hurray! Hurray! Give them two silver stars. Not!

This type of kindness and giving is self-serving. It may impress some people, but to those in the know, as they say, "they ain't foolin' anyone."

The greatest acts of giving go unheralded. You and God are the only ones that know about them. That's the way it should be. Some people call it being humble. I call it "humbility." It's the ability to be humble in giving situations.

At one point in our lives, my wife and I were flat broke and couldn't afford to buy groceries or pay our bills. I was too embarrassed to ask for help.

After feverish prayer and a few weeks eating those inexpensive noodles, someone anonymously left us an envelope with five one-hundred dollar bills at our church. Because someone was kind enough to give without expecting anything in return, we made it through that rough period in our lives.

I know that someday, if not already, the money will come back to those people who helped us in such a profound way. It was a strong gesture of "humbility."

The act of giving should not be shouted from the highest hill. Don't tell friends or neighbors. Don't make it a stunt or an event. Don't call the local newspaper. Don't announce it. Don't let anyone know.

Give to others and don't breathe a word of it to anyone. Trust me, you won't need the praise from others to make you feel wonderful about your gift.

When it really comes down to it, you can honor yourself and others with your simple goodness—not by your seeming greatness. There are two words that are often used in the Bible: Be humble.

Good advice for one and all.

Nothing warms the heart like quiet giving.

Everyone needs kindness

Kindness creates more kindness. When people are kind to you, you want to return the favor. But what about those that haven't done anything to earn your kindness? Why should you be nice to them? After all, some people don't merit kindness. Or do they?

The answer is quite simple. Sincere kindness isn't about the worthiness of a person. It's not about how he or she acts or is. It's not about good deeds. Sincere kindness means doing thoughtful and considerate things for people even when they don't deserve it. Come to think of it, those who don't deserve it generally need it the most.

Be kind to all.

Give more

Most people think if they give too much, they'll have nothing left. Just the opposite is true. The more you give, the more you'll receive.

Ever hear about reaping ten times what you sow? It's true. Once the heart of giving takes effect, the following also holds true. The more you give, the more is given back to you. And the more you have to give.

There is a wonderful, supernatural law of nature that says three of the most desired things in life—happiness, freedom, and peace of mind—are always achieved by giving them to someone else. Why don't you give it a try?

When you become a giver instead of a taker,
you'll experience life in a whole new way.

A crack in the sidewalk

While preparing for a triathlon a few years ago, I was jogging down a cracked sidewalk and wasn't paying attention. All of a sudden, I tripped on an uneven part of the walk and was headed for the ground when I instinctively went into a safety roll, jumped right back up and kept going as if nothing had happened. The only thing I hurt was my pride.

While in the U.S. Marine Corps, I learned how to hit and roll to avoid being injured in a fall. That training helped me avoid kissing the sidewalk. Thank you, Staff Sergeant Wilson!

You've probably been tripped up by a mistake every now and then. (Unless of course you've spent your life in a vacuum!) Did you fall flat on your face—or did you roll and get right back up? Everyone makes mistakes—those who jump right back up excel in life and avoid falling on their faces.

Jump right back up after you make a mistake.

Think first, jump second

While vacationing in Pagosa Springs, Colorado, my wife and I wanted to go white water rafting. Unfortunately, the water was too low when we we're visiting in August. Not wanting to waste a gorgeous day and a majestic mountain river, we decided to go tubing—the poor man's alternative to rafting.

Tubing is fun, relaxing, and requires absolutely no skill. You sit on an inner tube and float through the water.

After going to a local tire store and purchasing a couple of tire tubes, we inflated them and donned our bathing suits, suntan lotion, and our smiles. We paid a local man with a pick-up truck to transport us and our tubes to a secluded spot a few miles up river.

He dropped us off and we headed to the riverbank. The clear blue water of the mountain river was beautiful, fresh, and inviting. We slowly slipped into the water. Then suddenly we stopped and jumped back to the bank. That's when it clicked. We'd made a forty-degree mistake. The water was so cold that it was numbing—literally. But what was a couple of dumb vacationers from Ohio supposed to do?

We did what any other crazy tourists would do. We decided to float down the river anyway. We jumped on our tubes and tried to keep our bodies from touching the water. That seemed to work fine – at least for the first few minutes. Then we spotted the rapids about 200 feet ahead.

Yes, we survived, and no, we wouldn't do it again. At least not in freezing water.

Life can be a lot like that cold ride in beautiful Colorado. You jump into something—a relationship, job, financial decision, etc.—without first thinking about everything involved. You make quick decisions based on outward appearances. It's just a part of life.

If Jean and I had evaluated the situation before throwing caution to the wind, we would have realized the inviting, clear blue river was flowing from the top of the snow-covered Rocky Mountains. We would have also thought about the fact that inner tubes have holes in the middle. We could have avoided a couple of numb rear ends.

Whether you're considering a job change, thinking about lustful desires, or making an important financial decision, you need to think before jumping in.

Things are not always as they appear.

Put it in writing

If you've ever received a hand-written letter from someone, you know how special it makes you feel. Whether it's a letter of appreciation, a thank you card, or a love letter, chances are you hang on to that letter.

A hand-written letter is more than a how-are-things-going missive. It shows the recipient you care and you are sincerely conveying a personal and permanent expression.

Lately, most people have become very technically inclined. It seems that computers, telephones and other various technologies are trying to replace the very essence of personal communication.

You use e-mail instead of using what has come to be known as "snail mail." You call instead of visiting. You send a mail-merged letter to someone because it's faster and easier. Technology is fast making this an impersonal world. That's all the more reason for taking time to actually *write* a letter.

A letter written by hand is much more personal than the quick mail you have come to accept as a part of the age of technology. It shows you care about a person in a special way.

How many times do you read every last word of a type-written mail-merged letter that arrives in your mailbox? Not often, because you probably think it's junk mail. How many times have you received a hand-written letter and read the entire thing? More than likely, you browse over the typewritten letter but read every last word of the one written by hand.

You can do yourself and someone you know (or don't know) a favor by sending that person a hand-written letter. It's a win-win situation. I encourage you to write a letter today. You'll feel great for writing it and the recipient will feel great for receiving it.

Maybe someone has been a great friend and you want to express your appreciation. Maybe you just want to tell a loved one how much he or she is appreciated. Perhaps someone in a store helped you in an exceptional way, or a co-worker helped you with something. Maybe a receptionist does a fine job answering the phone or taking messages. Maybe it's a long-term customer you can reach out to and express your gratitude.

A hand-written letter can be about the little things or the big things. Regardless of the kind of letter—a simple thank you, a letter of appreciation, or multiple-page love letter—just take the time to write it by hand. It will be time well spent.

People love personal communication.

"When you make a mistake, admit it. If you don't,
you only make matters worse."

--Ward Cleaver

"Great people are not made by getting
the best of others, but by giving more
than they pay in return."

CHAPTER

10

Dealing with others

Changing others

If you want to change others, you must first be what you want to see in others. Most people have this backward. They think they have to change the other person before they change themselves. Wrong.

If someone in your life is causing you stress, then you've become a victim of a victim. You need to rise above it and not let it affect your life. You need to be a strong example of what you want others to be—you need to inspire them. When you inspire, others want what you have.

Instead of thinking about how you're going to change everyone around you, you must first make the changes in your own life. Others will follow.

Change others by setting the example.

Value others

Are you critical of other people? If you are, then why? Is it because it makes you feel better about yourself if you talk about others? You know you shouldn't belittle others, but you do it anyway. It's human nature.

When others have done wrong, are facing conflicts, or are ruining their lives with bad decisions, it's easy to focus on the bad and find all their faults.

The hard part is to look beyond the deed or action, look deep into the person and find that little spark that will rekindle the goodness in which they were born. Everyone has something valuable inside themselves. Sometimes they need your help to find it.

The best way you can help them is to take a sharing, caring, and encouraging approach and communicate positive things. After all, don't you want what's best for them?

Look for the true value in people.

Bite your tongue

What you say and what you *don't* say are equally important. To avoid conflict, you must know what to say and when to say nothing.

If you're like everyone else, you have a natural tendency to yell back at others who yell at you. There are times you want to settle the score or get even. You think you have the right to lash back with your tongue—and sometimes your fists.

Words spoken—or actions taken—in anger can destroy in minutes a relationship that took years to build. But it doesn't have to end that way. There's an alternative to lashing out.

Don't fight fire with fire. Try a friendlier approach next time. Bite your tongue and show kindness, calmness, and forgiveness. I didn't say it would be easy to fight the natural tendency to talk back with bitter words. In fact, it will likely be one of the hardest things you will ever do. But if you do, it'll prove you to be a much better person.

This response—or non-response—will not only have a profound effect on the person who is temporarily your adversary, it will make a better, more positive person out of you. It's a win-win situation.

The uncontrolled tongue can do severe damage.

Know-it-alls don't know it all

I've been to hundreds of breakfast/lunch/dinner meetings over the years. I like to listen to other people at the table. But I often keep my opinion to myself unless I'm asked to share. I also won't tell someone they're wrong—unless it's something I feel deeply about. It's simply not worth it. I prefer to sit back and listen to see if I can learn something new.

One day I had lunch with two CEOs and a salesman in Cleveland. There was an obvious distinction between the two successful men and the know-it-all salesman. The topic of selling came up and the salesman decided he would explain to me the right way to sell. I was all ears.

As a salesman with more than 15 years of selling everything from mortgages to fiber optics, I always like to listen intently to the people who think they have the world in their hands—especially salespeople. It reminds me of what not to do.

Here are some of the things I have learned:

- If you give a know-it-all a few minutes, you don't need to stick a sock in their mouth. He or she will have already stuck their whole foot in there.
- The know-it-all always has to be right. Don't play that game. Just act like you're listening. Smile and

nod your head a few times when it's appropriate. They'll never know the difference. They're too much in love with themselves to care.

- They'll brag about themselves early and often. Great people don't have to brag about themselves—it's apparent in all they do.

I didn't pay much attention to what was coming out of the guy's mouth that day. If he was as good as he thought he was, people would be working for him instead of the other way around. In other words, he'd be a CEO.

The guy wasn't a bad person. I just preferred the company of the other two men and my chicken sandwich.

Most of the time it's better to listen than to open your mouth and insert your foot.

CHAPTER

11

For men only

A lesson in memory

Women are more likely to remember special occasions than are men. It's not because they have a better memory. It's because they are more sentimental.

The easiest way to remember your wife's birthday or anniversary is to forget it once. But I don't recommend it! Write everything down. I started doing that and now I no longer shop for my wife the day before our anniversary. I write everything in my schedule a month or so in advance so I can prepare and plan.

For those who don't use a schedule or an organizer, there's still hope. Write a note and put it where you'll be sure to see it. (No need to thank me. We're in this together.)

Write things down and avoid the grief.

Twelve roses are better than a dozen

It took me a few years, but I finally figured this one out. Twelve and a dozen are not always the same thing.

Instead of sending that special person in your life a dozen roses all at one time, send a single rose a dozen times. When you send one rose every so often, you will leave a more lasting impression. Yes, it costs a few dollars more. Yes, it takes a little more time, but the rewards are numerous and ongoing.

In the long run—not just for one day—you'll give her more, twelve reminders that you care, not just one. Including a note, card, or gift that expresses how much she means adds a nice touch. Or you can take it one step further and write letters of appreciation to tuck in with some of those roses. It will be worth it—all the way around.

Show her you're <u>always</u> thinking about her, not just on Valentine's Day.

I almost bought a lawnmower for my wife

Ask 100 women if they would be happier cutting the grass or having their husband do it for them? Total the results. Any questions?

A lot of men these days lead their household the way the bully rules the playground--by dictating, domineering, and demanding; and by forcing their wives to serve them. These guys see it as macho. Show me one of these marriages, and I'll show you a disaster. Successful marriages aren't built on this horrible philosophy.

At one point in my marriage—before I wised up—I thought Jean wasn't doing a good job as a wife. I kept trying to figure out how I could change her so she would be more to my liking. How could I mold her into what I wanted and train her to my way of thinking? It took a while, but it finally hit me. This was the wrong way to approach the situation.

When I finally realized that I couldn't lead by demanding, I changed my attitude. I became a more serving, loving, and kind husband. I went beyond the call of duty—serving her like never before with emotional encouragement and acts of kindness. I poured on the love. I developed an attitude of serving her without expecting anything in return. I put her needs and desires ahead of mine.

120

A funny thing started to happen. I began to *enjoy* serving her. And guess what? I didn't realize it immediately, but she started to serve me more and more and love me more and more. The more I did for her, the more she did for me. As we fed off of each other, my attitude did a 180-degree turn.

I know it doesn't seem like the macho thing to do, and it's hard for you to admit that you serve your wife—especially around other men. (It's that macho image thing rearing its ugly head again.) But if you want a joyful and fulfilling relationship, you should serve.

And if you're still thinking about buying that lawnmower for the wife, don't.

Whether it's in a home or work relationship, serving others pays big dividends.

Happy wife, happy life

When the woman in your life is happy and feels appreciated, your relationship will flourish. On the other hand, if she's unhappy and doesn't feel appreciated, your relationships can wither and die. Think of a relationship as a flower and appreciation as sunshine. Without adequate sunlight, the flower will perish.

I'm not suggesting it's your responsibility to make someone else happy. I believe it's up to each individual to create happiness. I'm suggesting that you put some effort into making your wife feel appreciated.

Think about how it makes you feel when someone—a fellow employee, a friend, a relative—shows a sincere appreciation for something you've done. It feels great. Doesn't your wife deserve to feel the same way?

The first few years of my marriage, it seemed we were eating out all the time. I enjoy going out for a good meal, but there's something special about a home-cooked meal that I cherish. Over the past few years, I started thanking Jean for preparing meals. I know it's a huge sacrifice of time and energy in addition to everything else she does for our family. I sincerely appreciate it and value her efforts, and she deserves to know it.

You guessed it. When I expressed my appreciation for the wonderful home-cooked meals, Jean started cooking more and making a wider variety of dishes. When she realized that her efforts were appreciated, I sensed that she was enjoying cooking like never before.

Appreciation is a powerful tool. People respond in positive ways when they feel valued. Both Jean and I genuinely respect each other and try to never take one another for granted. We love to do things for each other, not because we're obligated to do so, but because we realize the other's worth.

If you're already showing your wife loads of appreciation: Keep it up!

If you're a person who could do better, it's never too late to start. Ask yourself, "What can I do to show more gratitude?" Most of the time, the answer is two little words: "Thank you."

When you constantly say thank you and mean it in a sincere and kind way, relationships benefit. A happy wife translates into a happy life. Don't believe me? Try the alternative.

Show her appreciation and she'll show you happiness.

"Happy marriages begin when we marry the ones we love, and they blossom when we love the ones we marry."

--Tom Mullen

CHAPTER

12

For women only

There's strength in unity

How far did we run those days in the Marines? I'll never know, nor will I care. Day after day on those hills, valleys, and those long stretches of asphalt, we became mindless running machines. We were young. We were strong. We were proud recruits in the United States Marine Corps.

Sweating at four o'clock in the morning, in formation, singing to a cadence, might not sound like a whole lot of fun to you. But trust me, it was. There was just something about teamwork that kept everyone going. The entire platoon—working as one—was accomplishing things we'd have never thought possible if we had to do them alone.

One of the greatest lessons those drill instructors taught us is that if a fellow Marine falls or lags behind, someone must be there to help him—to pick him back up and stay with him through the tough times. They taught us that having a buddy system might someday save our lives.

The journey of life gets tough sometimes. The hills, the valleys, and the long stretches of highway seem endless. Although I'm not a woman, I don't think I'm climbing out on a limb when I say that it probably isn't easy being one today.

But, ladies, allow me to offer an ounce of encouragement. You don't have to do it alone. For years, women have been haunted by the myth that "a strong woman stands alone."

How does a woman learn to be a great wife, mother, provider, and friend? By walking with other women who pursue the same goal. Sincere friendship is not just one more option to be added to an already impossible list of responsibilities. It is the means to accomplish that list. Here are four reasons why there is strength in numbers:

1. Shared strength: You can resist things together and fortify your position.
2. Shared support: You will lift up each other in trying times.
3. Shared encouragement: You'll keep each other going.
4. Shared effort: You'll have a much better return on your labor.

Find friends—fellow recruits—that share the same beliefs, and the biggest worries and intractable problems will seem less daunting. As for singing in cadence and running at four o'clock in the morning, that's entirely up to you.

A rope made up of two or more strands is stronger than a rope made up of one.

10 Ways to a man's heart

1. If you want more love, do more loving.
2. Remember that encouragement works. Nagging doesn't.
3. Tell him how much you appreciate him.
4. When a storm comes along, drop anchor and wait, the sun will come out tomorrow.
5. Ask him how you can make his life better.
6. Allow him freedom to enjoy his sports, cars, hobbies, etc.
7. Let him know that he means the world to you and that you'll never leave him.
8. Give him small expressions of your affection.
9. Give him a massage for no reason.
10. Pray for him.

It is always another's heart that makes you feel your own.

CHAPTER

13

For new parents only

Positive marriages speak volumes

Just like great companies that excel under positive leadership, your home will operate more smoothly when the environment is encouraging and your marriage is flourishing. Creating a positive emotional climate starts at the top. Children learn from their parents. You need to pay attention to what your marriage is saying to them.

Your children know when you argue, when you treat each other poorly, and when there is a problem in the home. A child's behavior is generally related to the environment in which he or she lives. When the insistent pressures of marriage start dictating the atmosphere of your home, your children will sense it and behave accordingly.

Many parenting troubles are actually marital troubles in disguise. Too many couples overindulge their children at the expense of their marriage, and their children experience problems as a result.

As a couple, you need to focus on each other's needs first, not those of the children. As an example, when you come home from work you need to spend time with your spouse *before* you spend time with the children. Gently tell the children, "I'm going to spend a few minutes with your Mother or Father because I love her or him and want to be with her or him…then we'll play together."

Initially, children might resist and complain, but that will change. When your children see a wonderful and loving relationship, they will feel much more secure. And security—at least to children—is what matters most.

As a parent, you need to have a positive loving marriage. If you give the impression that your marriage might fall apart, it's scary for the children. If you want them to feel secure, you should work on every aspect of your marriage to set a shining example of unity.

So how do you create an environment in which your kids can enjoy life and thrive? How can you set an example that your children will follow?

- Talk to one another and create harmony and an unwavering love for each other.
- Go to the library and check out some books focusing on positive relationships. There are literally hundreds of great books on the subject.
- Talk to other successful parents.
- Take positive action.

What are you waiting for? Your children are watching. Show them how love transforms a couple of devoted individuals into a team of individuals devoted to each other.

Love is the emotional glue that holds a family together.

Cherish the simple things

It isn't necessary to spend all kinds of money to have a great family life. Children love simple and repetitive activities. Anyone with young children, knows exactly what I mean. They want to read the same stories over and over, hear the same jokes hundreds of times, and play the same games forever.

What many parents don't realize is that many times children have more fun interacting with them than they do playing with expensive toys or going to special events.

If you were to ask most adults what their fondest family memories were from childhood, what would they say? Would it be the extravagant vacations, expensive toys, amusement parks, carnivals, or the zoo? Some would say yes, but the majority would say no.

Most children remember the simple things such as singing in the car, hiking to an old fishing pond, throwing the ball in the backyard, playing pretend, or just having fun on the living room floor. Remember those days?

You can't buy your way out of parenting responsibilities. So why do most people try? Busy and exhausted parents, especially those with plenty of money, sometimes attempt to pay off their attention-deprived kids with expensive toys and costly experiences. It doesn't work.

What children want most is to spend *quality* time with you—enjoying the simple things in life. There's no toy, roller coaster, bike, or day care center that could ever compete with the positive, fun interaction with Mom and Dad.

Simple cherished interactions with your children will be remembered for a lifetime.

The first three years...

The first three years of a child's life are extremely important. It's critical that you as a parent, provide a strong foundation of discipline, happiness, and core values during these years.

Ever watch someone plant a new tree? The ground (home) is carefully prepared to support the seedling (baby). The tree is fertilized and watered (fed). Tie downs (parents' discipline) are carefully wrapped around the tree to hold it steady and help it grow straight and tall. Often a special wrap (love) is placed around the base of the tree to protect it from hungry animals (negative influences).

As the tree matures, the tie downs are adjusted to allow the tree to grow. Sometimes they need to be tightened. Other times they need to be loosened. The tree is continually nourished with fertilizer and water and nurtured by nature's warm rays (happiness). By the time the tree is about three years old, it is on its way to acquiring a strong root system (core values) so that one day it won't need the support from the tie downs.

The strong root system that began to develop when the tree was but a seedling will someday allow it to provide shade and shelter for the one who planted it (you). All of the hard work and tender loving care that went into giving the tree a good start in life will be repaid many times over.

It's up to you to prepare the way for a child and to be there to guide and support the child until he or she is strong enough to go it alone.

Successful parents begin planting the seeds of success even before the baby is born. It might not be easy work, but in the end it will be among the most rewarding things you will ever do.

Today's seedlings are tomorrow's strong trees.

Extend 'tuck-in' time

Studies show that most parents spend less than three minutes tucking their children into bed. Did you know that children are most receptive at night and in particular just before bedtime?

My wife and I spend time with our children each night praying, talking, and telling stories. Extending tuck-in time allows us to give the affection we may have not had time for during the day. It enables us to look back at the wonderful events we shared and encourage them to look forward to a brand new exciting day in the morning.

Tuck-in time is when you have their undivided attention. If you want to improve your relationship with your children, I encourage you to take a few more minutes out of your evening to enjoy the wonderful bonding that takes place during those precious minutes.

You can start tonight!

CHAPTER

14

Make the most of your time

You have plenty of time

When is the last time someone told you they had plenty of time on their hands? Not lately, I'll bet. They're busy. You're busy. I'm busy. We're all just too darn busy.

Most people who lead busy, overcrowded and over-stressed lives have made the choice to do so. They just don't realize it. Some people say they don't have time for this or that, but what they're really saying is they have other priorities—they've made other choices.

The problem is in the priorities, not limited time. There's nothing wrong with having priorities. Complaining to others about the choices *you* make, however, may land on deaf ears.

Time hasn't changed, you have. 'Till the day you die, you'll have exactly 24 hours in each day—the same amount of time you had when you came into this world. Think of time as an endless supply that never runs out—because it never does (until you die, of course).

Unless you're behind bars in a government facility or a member of the military, what you do with your time *is your own choice.* (And even then, it's generally your choice; you wound up behind bars or in the service because of choices you made.) It's self-management, not time-management. You need to make more desirable choices. You need to decide what's important and what's not.

When it comes to your time management, make better choices.

"People who make the worst use of their time
are the same ones who complain that there
is never enough time."

--Anonymous

'No' makes you feel good

Wouldn't it be nice if you could live your life the way *you* want? Wouldn't it be nice to do the things *you* want to do? Guess what? You can and it's not hard. You must develop your "no" muscle. How is that done? By developing your "yes" muscle so it will work for you—not for everyone else— first. If you say yes to all the things that are important to *you*, then saying 'no' to what's not important will get easier and easier.

Here's how it works. Suppose you plan to take your children to the park this weekend—no specific time, just some time this weekend. When someone wants to borrow your time this weekend, it's not a problem telling them 'no' because you already have an obligation. When they ask you, just tell them you've already made a commitment or you're busy. It's really quite simple.

You need to set your schedule and rearrange it to fit *your* desires. It doesn't matter what it is—spending more time with your children, enjoying a hobby, going somewhere with a friend, or just reading a book. You need to set aside time to do the things you love and with the people you love.

When you do that it becomes very easy to refuse those who try to borrow your time. It's more difficult to tell someone 'no' when you don't have plans or haven't set goals for what you want to do. Planning ahead allows you to live your own life the way you want to live it. It allows you to focus on what's most important to *you*.

Learn to say "yes" to the things you love, and "no" will be much easier.

CHAPTER

15

Goals and dreams

Dreams are possibilities

You can imagine and dream about anything. But you must do more than that if you want to fulfill your desires. If you continue to only dream, that's all you have—dreams.

However, the moment you open up to the idea that a dream can become a reality, you've created a possibility. Once you see the possibility, your mind can start to cross that bridge over the chasm that, too often, you let separate your dreams from reality.

And once you start to cross that bridge, it's only a matter of time before you arrive at your desired destination.

See the possibility in all that you do.

"I'm convinced that one of the greatest
things you can do for people is to encourage
them to believe that there are no limitations."

Seek positive people

If *you* don't believe in yourself, who will? You are responsible for the life you lead. Only ten percent of life is about circumstances. The other ninety percent is about how you react to those circumstances and what you do about them. If you're tired of your lousy life, you need to stop crying and start creating the life you want.

I'm all about simplicity, humor, and living life to the fullest. I'm an average person. I've learned the hard lessons that experience teaches. For years, I pouted about why bad things have happened to me, and why I didn't have a good and happy life.

Then reality hit me in the face: People don't care about someone else's sob story. They don't want to hear about someone else's troubles. They've got enough of their own.

I realized it was up to me to create the life I wanted, and not allow myself to be formed by things around me. I stepped into the life I'd always dreamed of living and started to enjoy every minute of it.

I'm willing to bet there's not much difference between myself and millions of others out there—people who are pouting about what they don't have and what someone else does have. I encourage you to take a hard look at the life you're living and decide if that's *truly* what you desire.

The great Zig Ziglar always says that if you continue to do the same thing you've been doing, you'll get the same thing you've gotten. If you need proof, all you have to do is look at your own life and the lives of those around you. Successful people have consistently improved their lives in many ways. They don't continue to do the same thing *if it isn't working*.

If you're not where you want to be, it's no one's fault but your own. You must improve your situation. You must take a different path.

How do you change your life? Where do you find that path to a better life? Reading books like *Life Positive* is a good start, but it's not enough. You must make a decision to change deep within your heart, set goals, change your habits, change your attitude, build your character, consistently devour good information, and associate with positive people. And above all, you must take action.

Some years ago, I let go of most of my goals and dreams. I began to settle for mediocrity. Then one day, my motivation and dreams became real again. I met Scott Brown, author of *Service with Purpose*. Scott was a lot like me before he wrote his book—full of dreams, aspirations, goals, and a desire to excel in life. We shared some of the same ideas and philosophies. To some extent, we both lacked—or thought we lacked—the ability to take action.

We began to talk frequently and encourage each other to take action on our goals and dreams. Scott was, and still is, an inspirational source of encouragement. He's a great person to be around. He's the kind of guy everyone needs in their life. *Life Positive* is the result of my finally taking action. It's the result of having a friend in Scott, someone who encourages me to be more and is a positive influence in my life. I'm blessed to have met him.

If I can do it, you can, too. Stuck in a rut? Need some encouragement? Seek out people who can guide, encourage, and help you. It's easy to spot these people. Look for those who are joyful, uplifting, and who seem to have their act together. Get to know them. Ask for their advice, suggestions, and guidance.

When you start associating with positive people, their positive traits become contagious. You start to take on the same kind of characteristics. Unfortunately, the opposite is also true.

When you start hanging around people who always complain, who are negative, who are a bad influence on others, you tend to become like them. It's time to decide what you want out of life.

Associate with positive people and your life will take on new meaning.

Nothing can stop you

When it comes to goals and dreams, there are only five types of people:

1. People who don't care, have no goals, and don't commit.
2. People who don't think they can reach their goals, so they fear committing to them.
3. Those who have goals and dreams and believe they can accomplish them, but never take action.
4. People who take action on their goals but quit when adversity comes along.
5. Those who set goals, commit to them, and do whatever it takes to reach them without compromising their core beliefs.

Help yourself; be like the last one.

Goals mean nothing without action

A goal is something that stretches you to accomplish something you didn't think you could. Goals enable you to have a vision for your future.

It's easy to be drawn into meaningless directions by the pressures of today's society. When I recommend, "going for it" and "setting high goals," I don't mean falling prey to greed and destructive competitiveness. That type of hype will corrupt core beliefs and give you a false sense of commitment.

Also remember that goals are a dime a dozen. No goal-setter likes hearing that, but it's true. Goals take on value through strong belief and action. Most people fail to reach their goals because they make no sincere commitment, and they don't take action. These two ingredients are key.

Have a conviction (regarding your goals) and take action.

"A useless life is an early death."

--Johann von Goethe

"Great minds have purposes, others have wishes."

--Washington Irving

"The man who rows the boat
doesn't have time to rock the boat."

--Unknown

CHAPTER

16

Tidbits, short stuff,
quickies, and misc.

Stop playing the violin

Stop complaining about everything—other drivers, bad
weather, the boss. Make an honest effort to not complain for
one full day. You may be surprised by how you feel. But be
careful. It could become a habit.

Surprise someone

When you go through the trouble to plan a surprise and
spend the time and energy seeing it through, it shows you truly
care. Most people love surprises and that should be reason
enough to surprise someone today.

Say 'Hi' or wave

Whether you're at work, at the store, walking, or exercis-
ing, you should make it a habit to say "Hi" to everyone you
come in contact with. Even when you're in the car you can
wave to strangers—pedestrians, other drivers, and passen-
gers. It'll be fun, and spread a feeling of goodwill. It might
seem like that little wave has changed the world.

Everyone will seem friendlier. Truthfully, the world will not
have changed. People are just responding to positive behavior. It's amazing how easily you can change your attitude and
the lives of those around you for the better.

Change shoes

The next time you disagree with something another person is saying, stop, put yourself in their shoes and listen to what they are *really* saying. Make it a point to see what they see, feel what they feel, and try to understand their point of view.

You've been told this before, but when was the last time you actually did it?

It's all about the 'wuv'

One of the most touching things I've ever experienced was when my two-year-old son said, "I wuv you Daddy" while looking into my eyes. My heart fell to the floor. It wasn't until a few days later while driving to work that I realized how special those words were. I broke down and began to cry. I finally realized what parenting is all about.

It's not about how well they know their ABC's. It's not about how cute they are. And it's certainly not about the toys. It's all about the' wuv'.

An apple a day keeps the doctor away

What if this is true? Are you eating your fruits and vegetables?

Tom, Dick and Harry

Aren't you tired of people trying to get by with the least amount possible? People are saying to themselves "What is the least I can do to save my marriage?" "What is the least I can do to keep my job, get into heaven, or to perform any task?" Some people want to know what is the least they can do to survive. It's sad.

I hope this isn't you, because if it is, you're stuck with mediocrity, like Tom, Dick and Harry.

Life is about *thriving*, not surviving. If you look at the history of the world and study all of the winners in life—the legends, the champions, the great saints, and the great leaders—guess what you'll find? None asked themselves: "What is the least…"

Olympic competitors are the some of the greatest athletes in the world. If they said to themselves, "What can I do to just get by", would they ever have a chance of winning? Not likely. They train and prepare for years. They ask themselves what is the *most* they can do and they go out and do it.

Winners in life never settle for mediocrity. Whether they're spreading the gospel, serving customers, leading an army, helping a friend, or working on their marriage, winners always ask themselves, "What *more* can I do?"

Get rid of the poison

You don't eat poison, do you? I hope not. Most people don't eat poison unless they're trying to do themselves some serious harm. Anytime you put junk in your system, you're hurting yourself. Some people do it day in and day out but don't seem to realize it. Do you feed your mind with all kinds of destructive things?

I'm not a doctor, but I know this much: Flooding your mind with negativity can't be good for you. But you do it every day. How? By letting everything else decide what goes into your head—television, newspapers, musical groups, negative friends, etc. You don't control the incoming messages. You let someone else do it for you.

Want to enjoy a more positive life? Stop feeding your mind with poison!

Make a change, and have fun

Change something in your life today. Just for one day, change something and have fun with it. Change your name. Change your hairstyle. Change the way you get to work. Change your attitude. Change your underwear.
Just change something.

Seek wisdom

Everywhere you look there's opportunity. It may not fall in your lap, but all you have to do is drive around and you'll see opportunity calling out. Whether it's on a billboard, coming from your television, screaming from your radio, or popping up on your computer screen, it's all over the place. *Save money! Get rich in 5 days! Lose 30 pounds in 10 days*!

The problem isn't the opportunity. Opportunity is abundant and cheap. And as the saying goes, you usually get what you pay for. What you truly need is wisdom to sort through these so-called opportunities.

The thing to remember about wisdom is that it leads to good judgment, which allows you to make good choices. And if you're able to make good choices, you'll be in better shape to sort through the valuable opportunities that appear.

8 Don'ts for a good friendship

Don't hold your pride. Ask for forgiveness.

Don't bring up problems and mistakes from the past.

Don't yell at another person unless there's a fire.

Don't accuse, critcize, or complain about someone.

Don't be too busy when the someone needs help.

Don't forget to say "I'm sorry."

Don't expect perfection.

Don't forget: It takes two to fight, but only one to stop it.

"Life is really fun, if we only give it a chance."

--Tim Hansel

CHAPTER

17

Life is a big question mark

Life can be short or life can be long

I grew up on the shores of Lake Erie, but I never really got excited about fishing. But, my stepfather loved fishing for perch and walleye.

After I moved to Myrtle Beach, South Carolina, my family came for a visit. We decided to go deep-sea fishing in the Atlantic Ocean. While we were out there, the boat engine was sputtering a little, but nobody thought anything about it. We had a great time and my family went back to Ohio.

A week after our excursion, I heard that the very same boat we had fished on caught fire and sank in the ocean. I called my family to tell them and spoke with my stepfather. I remember we discussed how close we had come to death.

He finished the conversation by saying, "Ya never know, Tim." I agreed.

Life can be short or life can be long.

Ya never know.

Make the best out of every day of your life.

The cement truck theory

My theory about being a so-called workaholic—those who put their work before their family—goes something like this. Let's pretend you're married with children. One day at work, you cross the street and are accidentally run over by a cement truck.

Here's what comes next:

- At work: They're going to mourn your death and send your family flowers. Some will attend the funeral, and they'll talk about what a great person you were, and how they can't believe it happened. They'll wait a few weeks (sometimes not even that long) and begin the process of filling your vacated position. Yes, it was a sad loss, but the company has to move forward. It's business, and it has to be done. The world does not stop just because you are no longer there. That's just the way it is.

- At home: Your family and friends will also mourn your death, attend the funeral, and talk about how wonderful you were. But here's the difference: Your family's life will be turned upside down. They won't be able to replace you because you're not

161

just another employee. It'll be extremely difficult for them to move forward for some time. And in a relatively short time, most of your friends will return to their busy lives. But your family will still be trying to deal with your death.

Two weeks after I phoned my stepfather about the fishing boat incident and having the "Ya never know" conversation, he was run over by a cement truck. He was then life-flighted to the hospital in a helicopter. He died eight hours later.

My life, as well as the rest of my family's life, was turned upside down.

No one will ever know what he thought about in the closing moments of his life. But I'll wager that his thoughts were on his family and how much he cared about us. I'll also bet that he didn't even think about work.

Do I need to tell you how soon he was replaced at work? Do I need to tell you that he'll never be replaced at home?

You would be wise—and blessed—to spend more time with your family while you have them. You should also live your life as if today were your last day on earth—because it might be.

Ya never know.

Work can replace you, but you're family can't.

CHAPTER

18

Hi ho, hi ho, it's off to work you go...

Work can be addicting

Workaholism has become acceptable and even expected in many circles. So what's so bad about working longer and harder than the next person? Nothing, as long as it doesn't affect your family in a negative way and result in continuous problems.

What are the signs of workaholism? When you reach the point where you're spending too much time trying to figure out how to keep all your plates spinning and are unsuccessfully juggling your responsibilities, you're addicted. You're a workaholic.

Some people believe working extremely long hours is a must. I visited a freight company in Pittsburgh that had plaques on the wall for people who worked the most hours in a week. A senior-level employee actually took pride in having his name on the wall.

These so-called award winners may be doing well at work, but what about the rest of their lives? Is it really worth it?

I realize everyone has to earn a living, and I also believe there is dignity in an honest day's work. I've put in plenty of overtime during my life and worked long hours to meet deadlines. I'm all for it when it's needed, but when it's causing burnout and strain on relationships or other areas of your life, it's time to slow down, change patterns, and enjoy life.

When it gets to be too much, make adjustments. Do your family a favor and put them first!

Work smarter, not harder.

A pain in the neck

Ever get cut while shaving with a razor? Not pleasant is it? For millions of people, razor cuts are a part of life. The Gillette Company to the rescue. Gillette has been dominating the shaving market for years. Why? The company is continually improving its products. It's hard to think of ways to improve a simple razor, but Gillette does it.

In 1998, this successful company introduced the Mach 3, a triple-blade razor that replaced the two-blade model. Gillette claims there are 35 tiny improvements beyond the extra blade. In my experience (as well as millions of others), the Mach 3 virtually eliminates razor cuts that used to leave us bleeding. Small improvements, big results.

A pain-in-the-neck employee can be a lot like a razor cut. Unpleasant. If someone in your company is a pain, take a lesson from Gillette: improve, improve, improve. If the wayward employee doesn't like the idea of improving, show them the door.

Like the Mach 3, it'll put your company a cut above the rest.

Continually improve your products, your people, and your attitudes.

A 'pane' in the rear

Looking out one of the windows in the rear of my home, I notice things are distorted. The trees, the grass, my children, the bugs…everything looks different through this window. Why? It's wavy glass.

The window, like my house, is very old. The experts say the distortion is caused by an inconsistent thickness in the old window glass. To fix the problem, I need to replace the glass.

Looking at many people and companies in the world today, I notice things are distorted—customer service, attitudes, inconsistent philosophies, etc. An easy way to fix this wavy mindset is to get rid of the old way of thinking and invest in the new.

If I want to replace my old window with crystal-clear glass, it's going to take some time to custom build and install it.

The same goes for people and businesses. If thinking is distorted, it's time for a change. Replacing distorted thinking is not an overnight job, but the results will be much clearer (no pun intended) when you do.

If things seem distorted, it's time for a positive change.

A pane in the glass

Stained glass windows are beautiful works of art that have taken many hours of careful preparation, design, and assembly. Each window has multiple panes of different colors that are welded together to form the window. If any of those panes are broken or missing, it detracts from the overall appearance.

Likewise, in life or in business, broken "panes" can ruin the overall effect you get. If there's a problem employee, look for positive solutions for that person. If your attitude is bad about a relationship, change your attitude.

The beauty of life and/or business is that it is made up of the sum of its parts.

Fix your panes!

Words matter

Use your vocabulary, not to impress others, but to encourage them--to lift them up. Positive words can encourage someone to reach that next level, to change his or her mood and to live a more joyful life. Words that encourage and edify will be a blessing to others.

After speaking to a crowd of engineers at a convention in Charlotte, North Carolina, I felt as though I bombed. I thought I did a lousy job. I was upset with myself and wanted to hide in the corner.

After the speech, several people came up to me and thanked me for doing a great job. They thought I spoke with authority and conviction. Their comments lifted my spirit for the remainder of the day.

Have you ever been prompted to say an encouraging thing to someone and not followed through? I know I have. Many times, I've wanted to share a heartening word or two with someone and I neglected to do it. Don't do what I did.

If the thought of speaking an uplifting word to someone passes through your mind, let it flow from your heart.

Whether you think they need it or not,
encourage others early and often.

Do a self-check

Mike made a phone call from home one day. His side of the conversation went something like this:

"Mr. Bush please."

"Hi, Mr. Bush, I'm calling to see if you'd like to consider me as an employee. I'm a hard-working guy with unquestionable character and always have a positive attitude."

"Oh…I see. You already have someone working for you that fits that description."

"Is he always on time?"

"Are you pleased with his performance?"

"Do you plan on keeping him for long?"

"Well then, I'm glad he's providing you with a high level of satisfaction. Thanks anyway. Bye."

Over-hearing the conversation, Mike's mom said, "Mike, I know it's none of my business, but I thought that *you* worked for Mr. Bush."

"Yeah," said Mike. "I do. I just wanted to check up on myself and see how I was doing!"

It never hurts to check up on yourself.

Let's talk about job security

Ford Motor Company got rid of 5,000 jobs. Lucent cut 15,000 employees. Proctor and Gamble gave 17,000 staff members pink slips. In 2001, more than one million people lost their jobs.

It doesn't matter if you've worked for a company three days or thirty years, when it comes to job security—there's nothing to talk about. Business is business.

There's no such thing as job security anymore. You never know when you could be next to go. But if you are great at what you do, when one door closes, another will open. You'll never have to worry about a job.

Work like your job depends on it...it does.

CHAPTER

19

The leadership chapter

Lead, don't dictate

Want to know how to silence a room of executives? If you were in one of my seminars, you would hear me ask this question: "Why would anyone want to follow you?" You and I both know that you can't do anything in business without followers.

I'm sure you've heard the old saying "Lead, follow, or get out of the way." It implies that only aggressive, fearless people can lead. It also implies that you either step aside or jump in line. This isn't the way to lead. Ordering people around and living out your own little dictatorship isn't going to win the medal of leadership in today's world. Sorry.

Everyone knows that leaders need vision and energy. But to be great, all leaders need to serve. If you want to be respected by those you're in charge of and want to excel as a leader, you must take on the attitude of being a servant while still leading.

During my career, I've run across leaders both good and bad. I've also served in numerous leadership positions. What stands out in successful leaders is that they respect and contribute to the betterment of their followers. They'll jump in any situation headfirst and help any way they can any time they can.

I'll beat a path to the door of a leader who's willing to serve me and give me a reason to follow. The leader that relies on the theory of power, prestige, and intimidation will find themselves out the door without any followers.

Serve people and they will follow.

"Great leaders are not made by getting the best of others, but by giving more than they pay in return."

Focusing on the major things

Do you know who's the greatest blocking quarterback of all time? Me neither. Who cares how well a quarterback can block—except maybe occasionally his running backs?

In *The 21 Indispensable Qualities of a Leader*, John Maxwell—who I believe is America's foremost authority on leadership—shares the idea that a leader who knows his priorities but lacks concentration knows what to do but never gets it done. If he has concentration but no priorities, he has excellence without progress. But when he harnesses both his concentration and his priorities, he has the potential to achieve great things.

Over the years, I've worked with leaders that just didn't get it. They concentrated on the little things that didn't mean anything, instead of focusing on and developing their important strengths.

Take the quarterback for example. He's not likely to spend precious practice time learning to block. He's not expected to block; that's not his job. Blocking is not a skill that will help him as the leader on the field. Other players have the responsibility of blocking. The quarterback's strength is in his ability to throw the football. That's where he should focus most of his resources.

176

That's not to say you shouldn't work on some of the less important areas in your life. What it is saying is that you shouldn't make them a central point of your improvements.

How does one focus time and energy? John Maxwell encourages people to improve their focus by doing the following:

- Dedicate seventy percent of your time to your strengths.
- Delegate the insignificant things to others.
- Create an edge by investing time and money on what it would take to move to the next level.

The world of tomorrow belongs to the leader who can focus today.

CHAPTER

20

For the 'head honcho' only

It starts with the 'Big Dog'

Even those who are at the top can always learn. Here are seven steps to being a better "head honcho."

1. *Spend time in the trenches.* Not only will you gain the respect of your employees, but you will learn valuable lessons about your business that won't be found by reading *Fortune* magazine with your feet propped up on your desk. The best thing you can do is get involved. Spend a couple hours a month in the warehouse. Replace the receptionist for a few hours. Assemble a couple of products. Hop in the car and make a few sales. Experience what it's like to work for the organization from a different perspective. Talk to employees. Find out how to make their jobs easier.

2. *Encourage employee feedback.* Your employees should be your first priority--not customers, not suppliers, but *employees*. If you take care of your employees, everything else will fall into place. You won't have to worry about customers when your employees are treated with respect. Ask them what they want, how the business can improve, and what you can to do to become a better leader. The answers don't have to be anonymous. Let employees decide if they

want their names associated with the answers. You might be surprised at not only the answers, but also at how many people like to know their responses matter. Read the responses. Don't toss them in a drawer. Follow up the survey with a one-on-one session with each employee. Tell each about the basic direction of the company and get their input. Then use it to improve the company.

3. *Give Christmas/year-end bonuses.* The bottom line in the bottom line is the employees. A company doesn't get very far without them. Remember...it's a team effort. You need to reward your employees, or someone else will.

4. *Provide employee training.* One of the easiest ways to get a more productive and motivated workforce is to encourage employees to learn more about their jobs and seek self improvement. Allow them—in fact encourage them—to attend workshops, seminars, and various other productive training programs.

5. *Supply soft toilet paper.* The cheap stuff is like sandpaper. Need I say more?

6. *Offer sincere praise.* Notice I said *sincere* praise. There's nothing worse than false praise. But the old 'pat on the back' speaks volumes. A personal note or word of encouragement from anyone in upper

management to another employee is a great start.

7. _Don't be a "Work Scrooge."_ Allow employees the freedom to have fun. A "Work Scrooge" is a tough person to work for. Put someone in charge of organizing fun activities. Arrange to have potluck lunches. Bring in a comedian, speaker or entertainer once in a while. Make fun breaks as much a part of the routine as coffee breaks. Have a good time. Laugh and enjoy each day. People love to work for great organizations that allow some freedom. The business won't suffer. In fact, it will be better for the time spent having fun.

The successful, well-liked boss doesn't always spend his days in the ivory tower.

How to make your company irresistible

When people hire my consulting firm to help them with extraordinary customer service and business improvement, I'll always start by having them read this chapter of my book. Why? Because it starts to generate ideas. Please read on...

If people don't want to work for you, it's because you don't offer them anything they can't find elsewhere. You're the same as everyone else. Nothing makes you unique. Rather than mumbling about not being able to find good help these days or asking why no one wants to work anymore, you need to take a good look at your business. If you don't like what you see, it's time to make changes.

Great people are out there. But they're either self-employed or working for someone else, someone who offered something unique. If you can't make your workplace irresistible, then you probably can't get good help. On the other hand, if a company has the reputation of being a great place to work, resumes will come in by the basketful.

It's been repeated many times: Your employees are your greatest assets. But the question is: what are you doing to prove it? You can sit around and whine about the problems with the economy or the lack of a motivated workforce, or you can differentiate yourself from others and become a great company.

Phil Sakin is the president of Sakin Enterprises. His company's turnover ratio is below two percent *per year*. The company has 108 employees and is consistently growing. Sakin Enterprises has become an employer of choice. Why? Because Phil was tired of the turnover, bad attitudes, and his company's profitability, which he knew could improve.

Here's a few things he and his staff did to dramatically improve the appeal of the business to both employees and customers:

- He first asked for some outside (non-bias) help.
- He held a meeting with all of his employees from the filing clerk to the vice president. He shared his vision and asked them to take a week and think about improvements, ideas, and suggestions that would make Sakin a great company to work for. He received more than 179 suggestions. There was another surprise, too. Although a pay increase was near the top of the list, it wasn't the most important thing. Better working conditions and employee appreciation were in much higher demand. Although some of the suggestions couldn't be utilized, he met with his employees in groups and one on one to begin the transformation of Sakin Enterprises.

- One of the suggestions was to get rid of the voice mail system and replace it with a happy, living, breathing voice to greet customers. Customers raved about how nice it was to be able to talk to a real live person.
- He had the entire facility cleaned from top to bottom.
- He also cleaned house in a different way—he gave the 'rotten apples' their pink slips.
- He completely re-wrote his employee handbook to accommodate the employees' needs—not those of the company. Profit-sharing and employee ownership programs were put into place. He created bonuses for *all* employees when certain company goals were reached. Employees were granted more time off.
- He encouraged and sponsored personal development and customer service training.
- He met with all management and upper-level executives to ensure there would be praise and encouragement every single day.

When all was said and done, 48 improvements or changes were in place. And they paid off. Attitudes became positive. Productivity soared. Customer service became impeccable.

185

Sales and profitability skyrocketed. Sakin Enterprises became a place where everyone wants to work.

Sakin Enterprises isn't a lone ship in the night. Any company can join the employer-of-choice fleet. Here's five simple steps to get you started:

1. *First look for outside help.* Get *impartial* suggestions and recommendations.
2. *Improve your team.* Clean house. Get rid of those with bad attitudes. Hire winners.
3. *Change your core beliefs.* It's not what you say, it's what you believe in, commit to, and follow through on.
4. *Change your attitude.* Your employees should come first, not customers. When you put your employees first, they'll make sure your customers are taken care of.
5. *Put what employees want ahead of what you want.* Find out what your employees think will make your company exceptional and implement the positive suggestions.

When a company is irresistible, employees will come and profits will soar.

Ask exceptional people

If you have employees who have top-notch people skills—those who know the customers and can continually bring loyal customers back for more—you need to do what it takes to keep them happy and stay with the company. If you don't take care of them, your competitors will.

Great employees have standards higher than those listed in any job description. They also continually use their freedom to experiment, to embrace change, and to help move the company in an upward direction.

So how do you keep the great ones? Just ask them some direct questions. For example: "What can we do to keep you here?" and "How can we improve your job functions and work environment?" They'll give you the right answers.

Some companies try to "buy" a great staff. In most cases, this isn't the way to go. It's not only expensive, it's sometimes counter-productive. Most of the time you're left with a group of mercenaries, ready to leave for the highest bidder. Remember, nine times out of ten, money isn't the only factor.

Almost without exception, when exceptional people are taken care of, they don't think about leaving.

Exceptional employees are priceless.

CHAPTER

21

Take action

Get moving!

One of the secrets of getting ahead is getting started.

The secret of getting started is splitting up difficult tasks into smaller tasks and then taking action on the first one.

Remember, the way to eat an elephant is one bite at a time.

Being successful at anything doesn't happen overnight. It takes time, and it starts with one small task. Don't get mad if you don't get ahead overnight. Have a specific goal in mind so that your daily routine of moving into action takes on meaning.

Action begins with one small step.

"Goals will always be dreams, unless you take action."

Don't get too comfortable

One of the biggest lies this world has told itself over the last 50 years is that happiness, positive growth, and success are available without any effort or passion.

They're not.

Not putting forth the effort or having any passion generally means you're comfortable. The problem with being comfortable is that it rarely produces great results.

Want proof? Think of a few people who you feel have made huge contributions to the world. Look at their lives. They didn't live life in the comfort zone. They reached outside of their comfort zone to do things that everyone else fears. They stretched their efforts beyond those of ordinary people through courage and passion and achieved extraordinary results.

Undeniable courage and passion do not mix well with comfort. No positive growth has ever been made without effort.

If you're comfortable, you're not growing.

Get off your rear!

Your goals become meaningful only when you take action. But what if you never take action?

Fewer than five percent of the population actually set goals. Fewer than twenty percent of that five percent actually take action on those goals. That's what makes reaching your goals so rewarding. If it were so easy, everybody would be doing it.

But let me ask you again, what if you never took action on your goals? How meaningful and inspirational are they? Look at it this way: Let's say you decide to lose weight and get in better physical shape. So the first thing you do is buy a piece of exercise equipment. Then you schedule a day in which you'll start working out.

The big day arrives. You grab your workout clothes, your new exercise gadgets, your water bottle, and head to your workout area. But before you get there, you get distracted by something and end up doing nothing.

You have good intentions, but never take action. Then one day (months later) you realize you're putting on some extra pounds and decide to get in better shape—again. You're really going to try this time because you bought the fitness book (or video) to help. There's one problem though: you forgot you sold your get-in-shape-quick gadget in the garage sale with a sign attached that said "Never Used." It never fails. There's always some sort of fitness gadget or contraption selling for just a few bucks.

Positive action must be taken toward your goals. If your goal is to get in shape, you need to drop the junk food, get off the couch, and put some sweat on your body. Once you take that first step, you need to continue with two, three four, etc., until your goals are realized.

You're not going anywhere unless you take action.

Crossing the rickety bridge

Imagine a large canyon with turbulent water below and a roped bridge connecting two sides of that canyon. The bridge is very old and rickety. It's missing boards. It's shaky, and it looks unstable. Nevertheless, it's the only way to get across the canyon.

On the other side of the canyon are your success, hopes, and a wonderful life. Until you actually cross that bridge, you'll never get to the other side. Sounds kind of simple, doesn't it?

But think about it for a minute. How many times have you wanted to do something but never did because you didn't take action? You never crossed the bridge.

But let's change a few things. Imagine the same scenario, only this time you're going to cross the bridge. You know it will be a struggle. It won't be easy, and you may even lose hope and want to turn back. However, if you make it across that bridge, you'll enjoy a life that goes beyond your dreams.

Sincere and honest change always starts on the inside with a decision. You must first make the decision to do something, then take action.

Have you really made the decision to change your life? Do you think you're going to be successful? Get in shape? Improve your marriage? Spend more time with family? You've probably said these things year in and year out—yet how many changes have you made? There's a huge difference between deciding to change and actually doing it.

Here's a case in point. Three women are sitting in the lunchroom talking about improving their jobs. One of the ladies decides to be kind to all of her fellow employees. The next one decides she will take some classes on leadership. And the last one decides to really focus on being friendlier to customers.

Do you think the company benefited from these employees' decisions? Not hardly. Why? Because they didn't *do anything* about their decisions. Their decisions weren't sincere. They just talked about them. They decided to do something and *didn't* follow through. If they had taken action, they would have benefited tremendously.

I believe that when you don't make sincere decisions it's because you don't have a *reason* to actually do it. Why do you want to change? Why do you want to improve? Why do you want to succeed? Are you sincerely happy with the direction you're headed if you don't take action? What are the pros and cons of doing the same thing you've been doing?

Most people have a hard time answering these questions. Why? It's just not something you think about. However, because you want to move forward—you need to be setting goals. In other words, you need to be forward thinking. When decision time rolls around again, write your reasons down on paper and read them over and over.

People whose actions are forward-thinking are continually growing. They are always looking for and taking on new challenges and setting new goals. They're always creating, modifying, and thinking of ways in which they can improve. They don't ignore the past, deny it, or forget about it. They remember the last time they tried to cross the bridge and where the loose boards were so they can avoid them this time. They use their past to shape their future. They are also motivated by what the end result will bring them (forward-thinking). Additionally, they must focus on how they will reach those benefits (living in the present).

Forward-thinking people define where they want to go, use it as motivation, enjoy the present and focus their thoughts on how they are going to get there. While they're crossing that rickety bridge, they focus on where to make that next step and thoroughly enjoy the experience. They take in the view, and enjoy the journey, step by step.

When I began writing *Life Positive*, I sometimes became overwhelmed at the thought of everything I needed to do to complete the manuscript. But when I began looking past those missing boards in the bridge, I was motivated by the rewards of the completed book and so each step became much easier.

I knew that if I lived in the present and followed through

with my plans, I would cross the bridge and reach my goal. I thoroughly enjoyed writing the book. Even if I had never sold one copy, the journey would still have been wonderful and in my mind, it would have been extremely fulfilling.

When forward-thinking dominates your thoughts, it gives you a lot of reasons to accomplish what you want. You need to dig down deep and reveal those reasons. Why? Because when you mix your decisions with your reasons, you end up with a new passion. And with passion, your life will continually be transformed into what you have always wanted.

Isn't that your desire?

Let the past help shape and set your goals. Be motivated by the thought of reaching those goals. Enjoy the present. Take action.

The triple dog dare

The triple dog dare. Whether it was kissing little Sally on the cheek, telling your personal secrets, sticking your tongue on a frozen steel pole, or ringing the doorbell and running, the triple dog dare was always the most intense dares of them all. It challenged you as a kid to make a decision whether or not to listen to your self or give in to the peer pressure. Remember those days?

If you haven't figured it out by now, this is supposed to be a self-help book. At least that is what they label it in the bookstores. In other words, I'm doing my part—giving you positive information you can build on. The rest is up to you. I think that is why they call it *self*-help.

If you want to create lifelong improvements in your life, I encourage you to read the nuggets of wisdom contained in this book and share them with others. I recommend that you refer back to them again and again. When you begin to apply these ideas and strategies, the rewards and fulfillment will be never-ending. It's an incredible feeling.

What will you do? Will this information just fly right out of your head, or will you hold onto it and apply it?

This little book is meant to be an ongoing source of inspiration, something to refer to over and over. No matter how much you want to do good deeds for others, for example, you'll still need regular reminders.

Life Positive is meant to be an encouraging reminder. Pick it up and spend a few minutes reading to start your day or before you go to bed or anywhere in between. Hopefully, it will help you form new habits. Hopefully, you'll come away with just one thing that will help you live a much more fulfilling life.

I dare you to leaf through this book, find a principle or idea you want to practice, write it down, and take action.

No, I take that back, I triple dog dare you!

Live a positive fulfilling life!

"If you don't make a change in your life,
you won't make a change in your life."
--Unknown

INDEX

200

About the Author

Timothy Michael Olney is a husband, father, speaker, author, customer service guru, and down-to-earth guy—inspiring individuals and organizations to reach their full potential.

He knows the world is a great place, that nice guys finish first, and that anything is possible. His simple approach to positive living is described in the books and articles he writes. Tim's heartfelt desire is to help make this world a better place—both at home and in the workplace.

As president of Leaderbrook Publications, Olney speaks, develops and leads seminars, workshops, and training for individuals and organizations that desire extraordinary customer service and business success.

Olney is the founder and managing director of *Positive Boost Monthly*, the publication that is helping thousands of people enhance their lives—both personally and professionally—through positive living. He is also the creator of www.PositiveBoost.com which is fast becoming the #1 website for positive inspiration and life-changing content.

Tim Olney lives in Amherst, Ohio with his wife Jean and two children—Nathaniel and Kylie.

If you would like Tim to speak to your group or organization, or would like more information about his products and services, please visit his website at:
www.TimOlney.com

Tim would love to hear from you. Send him an email to:
tim@TimOlney.com

Or write him the traditional way and share your stories:

Tim Olney
P.O. Box 864
Amherst, Ohio 44001-0864

Give the gift of *Life Positive*
to your family, friends and colleagues

Check your leading bookstore or order here:

YES, I want _____ copies of *Life Positive* at $12.95 each, plus $3 shipping & handling per book. (Ohio residents, please add 5.75% sales tax per book.) Canadian orders must be accompanied by a postal money order or certified check in U. S. funds.

(Quantity discounts available— Please call.)

My check or money order for $ _____ is enclosed.

Leaderbrook Publications
P.O. Box 864
Amherst, OH 44001

or call today!
1-800-250-1636

or visit the website at
www.TimOlney.com